Recipes for Repair

A Lyme Disease Cookbook

Iced Minted Raspberry Green Tea, page 151

Recipes for Repair
A Lyme Disease Cookbook

Recipes and tips for the
anti-inflammation diet developed
by Dr. Kenneth B. Singleton,
author of *The Lyme Disease Solution*

By Gail Piazza and Laura Piazza

PECONIC
PUBLISHING, LLC

Book design and photography by Laura Piazza
Recipes written and developed by Gail Piazza
Copy edited and proofread by Elizabeth Urello

The text relevant to the Lyme Inflammation Diet® was adapted from
The Lyme Disease Solution, with permission from Dr. Kenneth B. Singleton.

Library of Congress Cataloging-in-Publication Data
Piazza, Gail; Piazza, Laura
Recipes for Repair: A Lyme Disease Cookbook :
Recipes and tips for the anti-inflammation diet developed by
Dr. Kenneth B. Singleton, author of *The Lyme Disease Solution*

Published by
Peconic Publishing, LLC, PO Box 265, Sunapee, NH 03782

Orders can be placed at www.recipesforrepair.com.

ISBN-13: 978-0-9830977-0-9
ISBN: 0-9830977-0-4
LCCN: 2010940023

1 2 3 4 5 6 7 8 9 10

Printed and manufactured in the United States of America
First Edition

Printed by TDS Printing Inc., Nashua, NH 603-882-4510

. . . .

Disclaimer: This book provides healthy and nutritious recipes and all information provided is for educational purposes only. All matters regarding your health, including changes in your diet, require consultation with a physician. Those who might be at risk from the effects of salmonella poisoning should consult with their doctor before consuming raw eggs. Neither the authors nor the publisher assume any responsibility or liability for any possible adverse effects resulting from the use of information contained herein.

. . . .

Dedication

This book is dedicated to the
chronically ill. It is our sincerest
hope that the information and
recipes within bring about
positive changes in your health.

Never give up your battle.

Acknowledgements

We would like to express our deepest gratitude to the following people for their pivotal roles in *Recipes for Repair: A Lyme Disease Cookbook*:

A special thank you to Dr. Singleton, for caring so deeply about your patients. It is clear your devotion to helping the Lyme community inspired you to write *The Lyme Disease Solution* and to create the Lyme Inflammation Diet®. We appreciate all the guidance you've given us, your support and your words of encouragement.

To Ursuline Singleton, MPH for sharing your nutritional knowledge, and for your support throughout the process.

To Elizabeth Urello, for your impeccable attention to detail, for always beating your deadlines and for exceeding our expectations.

To Paul Lindemann of Montage Marketing, for your enthusiasm, and for the outstanding work you've done for us.

To Allan Millstein, CPA, PC, for your expert advice and especially for being there for us, despite your already full schedule.

To March McCubrey and the crew at TDS Printing, for your guidance, and for your devotion to making sure all of your print jobs meet the highest of standards.

Gail's Personal Words of Gratitude

To my parents, who were such wonderful role models: you showed me by example how to succeed in life. Your love and support were never-ending.

To my husband, Jerry: how do you thank someone for always being there when needed, for never doubting your ability and for always encouraging you to reach your potential? Without your love and encouragement, my life so far would not have been such a rich, happy experience. Thanks for all you've done for me, especially over the past year when this book consumed not only my life, but yours. Jerry, thanks for being you.

To Gina, my "doctor daughter," for always being only a phone call or email away when I need your help and advice. Your many achievements and your devotion to your family, friends and patients are things we have all come to count on.

To Laura, my "partner daughter," for all of your unending work that made this book something we can both be proud of. Your attention to detail, graphic design skills and amazing photographic talents will be apparent to anyone who looks at this book. You bring the same love and spirit to everything in your life, which makes all of our lives so much better for having you part of our family.

To Chris, my "director son": your unique sense of humor, wit and artistic talent will surely make you a success in your career. But it is your kind, caring good nature that makes you such a pleasure to be with.

To my sister, Lynn, my special friend, who has been so important to me my whole life.

To my brother, Joseph: the older we get, the more I realize how important it is to have a big brother to count on.

To my son-in-law, Chris, for all the support you have given to Laura. You have helped her in so many ways to cope with the challenges that she's faced. This past year has been very demanding. Thank you for your patience and help.

To my testers: every recipe developer needs devoted, impartial taste testers who can tell it like they "taste it." Mine are the best. Thank you for your many years of service.

To my cousin, Diane, who is like a sister to me.

Laura's Personal Words of Gratitude

To my husband, Chris, for your love and unwavering support throughout the years. Despite the challenges I've had to face and the uncertain time line for recovery, you've always been there to reassure me that everything would be ok. There is no greater comfort to me than to know that I have you on my side. I appreciate all your support during the recent deadlines, and your helping me to remember to take time for myself.

To my mother: there are no words to express my gratitude for all you've done for me throughout my life. Your selfless nature of putting your family first turned the idea for this book into a reality. It has been such a pleasure to photograph your elegantly styled food. You've outdone yourself with these exceptional recipes and cooking and eating them has been my favorite part of this whole project.

To my father, for always being there for me and for your kind and generous nature. You have been so helpful, and I'm especially thankful for your understanding of my requiring all Mom's time these past few months! We could not have done this without you.

To my sister, Gina, and my brother, Chris: no matter how far apart we live, you are always in my thoughts. I am proud of you both, and I know we will always be there for each other, no matter where our lives take us.

To both Dr. Horowitz and Dr. Tallman-Ruhm, for everything that you do. You've educated me on how to support my body while it undergoes such challenges and you do so with such passion. Your devotion to your patients is clear, and I thank you for all that you do for me and others.

To David Hunter, for your commitment to helping those in the Lyme community, and for your words of encouragement over the past two years.

Thank You

Table of Contents

How to Use this Book

This book explains, and provides recipes and tips for, the Lyme Inflammation Diet®. The recipes are organized according to the four Phases of the diet, and each page has the following features:

with Brown Rice Pasta

...dard pesto, which is typically made
...e nuts. The inclusion of parsley,
...w dimension to this easy sauce.

...ok the pasta according to the package
...ections.

...ile the pasta is cooking, place all the
...maining ingredients, except for the oil, into
...ood processor and pulse until the herbs are
...mpletely chopped.

...zzle the oil down the feed tube and continue
...process until all the oil is incorporated.

...serve a tablespoon or two of the pasta water
...fore draining the pasta.

...ss the drained pasta with the pesto. If
...cessary, add some of the reserved pasta water
...thin the pesto. Serve immediately.

ASE 3 Variation: Once you reach Phase 3,
...can stir 2 tablespoons of grated Parmesan
...ese into the pesto before tossing it with
...pasta. Top the pasta with chopped plum
...atoes and additional grated cheese.

...pasta? Try this pesto as a topping for
...e to Homemade Mayonnaise (page 248)

 Indicates foods added, or shifted to earlier Phases, since the 2008 version of the Lyme Inflammation Diet® (pages 71, 109, 155 and 207)

🅐 **Category** indicates Breakfast, Soups/Salads/Sides/Snacks, Entrees or Desserts/Drinks

🅑 **Symbols** indicate support of the following dietary restrictions:

Gluten-free   Dairy-free   Egg-free   Vegetarian   Low sugar

Note: We interpret the following dietary restrictions as follows:

Gluten-free recipes may include oats.* Some oats are certified organic and gluten-free.
Read labels closely.

Vegetarian recipes don't include meat or poultry, but may include fish, eggs, honey and/or dairy products.

Low sugar recipes are low in sugar content and are in compliance with low-sugar diets for people with yeast concerns.

Dairy-free recipes do not include ghee, which is a dairy product, although in most instances, those who are lactose intolerant can eat ghee without ill effects. Any recipes that contain ghee as the only form of dairy can be adapted to be dairy-free by using the alternate oil suggested in the ingredients list.

🅒 **Phase** numbers are color coded as follows:
■ Phase 1 ■ Phase 2 ■ Phase 3 ■ Phase 4

🅓 **Title** and comments for the recipe

🅔 **Recipe time and serving size**

🅕 **Ingredients**

🅖 **Directions**

🅗 **Variations** of the recipe suitable for other Phases

🅘 **Notes** giving nutritional details or cooking tips

* According to the experts at www.celiac.com, recent research indicates that oats may be safe for people on gluten-free diets, although many people may also have an additional, unrelated intolerance to them. Cross-contamination with wheat is also a factor that you need to consider before choosing to include oats in your diet.

Cross-Referenced List of Recipes

Below is a list of the recipes in this book, cross-referenced by the following categories: gluten-free, dairy-free, egg-free, vegetarian and low sugar, as well as according to their Phase listing. If you have dietary restrictions, this list will enable you to quickly see which recipes are appropriate for your specific needs.

Foreword

What if I were to tell you that one simple thing can improve your energy and reduce your pain within hours, help you lose unwanted weight within days, and improve your mood within minutes? You might call it a miracle. Or maybe you'd call it a wonder drug.

And what if I were to tell you that this simple thing does not come from the medical field or the scientific community, is affordable to everyone and can be exceptionally pleasing to all five senses: taste, smell, sight, touch and even sound? You might say it was beyond miraculous.

Hippocrates said "Let food be your medicine, and let medicine be your food." How interesting that the father of Western medicine knew some 2,400 years ago that food is not only meant for basic sustenance, but also as medicine to cure disease and promote health.

Food is indeed very powerful medicine. Healthy food, tastily and pleasantly

Whole Wheat Pizza Dough, page 219

prepared, is especially powerful, because it heals both the body and the soul.

The book you're now reading, *Recipes for Repair: A Lyme Disease Cookbook*, is a guide to help you discover the healing power of healthy and tasty foods.

Today, an epidemic of chronic inflammation confronts us. After nearly forty years of practice as medical doctor (MD), I can say with great confidence that this outbreak is out of control. The list of serious disorders linked to chronic inflammation is extremely long, and it grows longer every day, with no solution or end in sight. Medicine does not yet have the right kinds of drugs to treat or prevent this scourge, nor does medicine have a good idea for how to prevent it.

Hippocrates knew the answer: food!

Fortunately, healthcare science is beginning to recognize the vital importance of nutrition. More and more published articles explain how foods can heal, and it is increasingly recognized and scientifically documented that food is a powerful influencer of health and disease.

As a board-certified specialist in Internal Medicine, I have worked a long time in the field of chronic disease care (the focus of over 85% of all healthcare spending in the United States). About twelve years ago, I discovered that I myself had Lyme disease. Since my recovery, which included gaining total control of all inflammatory symptoms, I have devoted much of my practice to helping other people with Lyme and similar tick-borne diseases regain their health by using the principles I learned through research and experience.

In treating patients with chronic Lyme and similar diseases, I have learned that proper nutrition is a critical factor in healing and recovery. Moreover, I discovered that an integrative approach to Lyme – combining conventional medicine, including antibiotics, with natural, holistic therapies – is the only way to fully reclaim your health.

Yes, regaining vitality and health is possible, and you should never give up hope. Remember that it's always too soon to quit. The odds of recovery are greatly increased once a patient with chronic Lyme disease takes responsibility for his or her own health, and makes a good approach to lifestyle – especially nutrition – a fundamental component of his or her recovery plan.

As a result of what I learned in my personal Lyme disease journey, combined with what my patients taught me over the years, I decided to write a book that would help others understand basic principles of Lyme recovery. That book is *The Lyme Disease Solution*, published in 2008. It is the first physician-authored, Lyme-oriented book to include at its core a truly comprehensive and integrative approach to Lyme disease recovery. Reflecting the impact of diet and food on Lyme-related chronic inflammation, I included a major chapter on diet and nutrition in the book.

That chapter, Chapter Five, recognizes the crucial role of nutrition in the healing process of Lyme disease, and integrates that information into a total program for recovery of health for Lyme patients. The chapter introduces the *Lyme Inflammation Diet*® (LID), which provides a wide-ranging nutritional program to reduce the inflammation induced by Lyme and other tick-borne diseases. It describes a multi-phase program to eliminate unhealthy foods and promote healthy, detoxifying foods, followed by slow reintroduction of additional healthy foods.

Thousands of patients have now tried the LID approach to nutrition with excellent results overall. In fact, according to patient response and feedback, the LID chapter has been perhaps the most helpful section in my entire book.

Several of my Lyme doctor colleagues now direct their patients to "read Chapter Five of Dr. Singleton's book" for a detailed approach to their nutrition needs. Patients, in turn, often say that it changed their lives. While there is no such thing as "one size fits all" when it comes to diet or therapy, about 75% of my patients say that the LID made a positive difference for them, and that they'll never eat the "old way" again.

Anthony is one example of the effectiveness of the LID nutrition program. He didn't really believe that diet could make much difference in his joint inflammation pain. Then he tried the LID, and was shocked by how eliminating two simple food types (gluten-containing grains and casein-containing dairy) dramatically reduced his joint symptoms. Incidentally, his gut symptoms also got much better. He said to me: "Gee, doc. I had no idea how much the bread and dairy were contributing to my symptoms. As much as I love pizza, I guess for now I'll have to let it go." He is right when he says "for now." Many patients are later able to reintroduce some foods to which they are sensitive, but only in a planned, phased-in manner over time.

Susan is another example. Like many Lyme patients, Susan struggled with weight control secondary to her Lyme disease. Susan drank eight to ten diet soft drinks a day. After reading Chapter Five of my book, she realized she needed to eliminate aspartame, the artificial sweetener in those drinks. Most people don't realize this particular sweetener can potentially produce neurotoxic side effects, especially upon exposure to heat. This can happen in part from aspartame's conversion to wood alcohol after consumption. Susan's email to me read, "Dr. Singleton, thank you so much for the LID diet and the other food principles in your book. I think you were right about aspartame. When I gave it up, my brain fog and my neuropathy began improving within days, and they are now much better! Keep up the good work helping us Lymies!"

As delighted as people have been with the LID chapter, it mainly provided an overview of healthy, anti-inflammatory dietary principles. While the LID chapter did include several helpful and delicious sample recipes, it was not a "how to" recipe book, per se. Overwhelmingly, people wanted more recipes, and they also wanted more LID-friendly food choices. Based on the feedback I received, it was also clear that Lyme-challenged people wanted recipes that were easy to follow, and that their families would also enjoy.

Thus, a recipe-based companion book to the basic LID was needed, with additional food options added to the program. Fortunately, as so often happens, the time must have been right. Soon after my wife and I began discussing the need for a new book to deal with these issues, I received a letter from Laura Piazza proposing a book that would meet that need. *Recipes for Repair: A Lyme Disease Cookbook* is the result.

In this book, Gail Piazza and Laura Piazza do a masterful job of developing dozens of delicious and beautifully presented recipes based on the principles of the Lyme Inflammation Diet®. The wonderful flavors and appearance of these tasty recipes are such that the entire family (not just the Lyme patient) will enjoy them.

Please keep in mind that the practical, affordable, expertly designed recipes contained in this book are for the repair and healing of chronic inflammation from *any* cause, not just Lyme disease or other tick-borne diseases. In addition, this book contains a much-expanded LID food list based on my consultation with the authors, as well as updated information about the LID program itself.

Now, please allow me to briefly introduce the authors and my friends, Gail and Laura.

Gail Piazza is a home economist with a Master's degree in Food and Nutrition from New York University. A highly experienced food expert, she has been producing delicious recipes and styling food for over 35 years for clients such as Emerilware, All-Clad and Farberware. Recently, she re-tested and reworked many of Dr. Andrew Weil's recipes, which were republished in a series of cookbooks for small electric appliances manufactured for Dr. Weil.

Gail is a published cookbook author, and has done recipe development and testing with other writers for ten cookbooks. Several of these are health-related, including a book focused on cancer-free living. Along with expert recipe development, Gail is also a food stylist whose work is seen in print, commercials and movies. She has styled food in thousands of attractive images for a very impressive list of clients, and her considerable talents are obvious in *Recipes for Repair: A Lyme Disease Cookbook*.

Gail's daughter, Laura Piazza, is a graphic designer and professional photographer with over ten years of experience. She has designed this book to present both health and food information in a simple, engaging manner, and has used her unique artistic skills to capture recipes in gorgeous color photographs. Incidentally, Laura is also a Lyme patient who has herself struggled with chronic inflammation, just like most chronic Lyme patients.

Food-based healing is possible, and *Recipes for Repair: A Lyme Disease Cookbook* is a wonderful resource to help you accomplish your healing goals in a way that's highly satisfying to all of your senses. Gail and Laura have created a book that is not only healthful, but also beautiful and easy to put into practice. Regardless of your likes and dislikes, you will find appetizing recipe solutions here. Try them, and I promise you won't be sorry. Monitor your progress, and it won't be long before you see the difference that these recipes will make in your life and in the lives of your family members.

Please enjoy this wonderful book, and taste the difference health can make!

Kenneth B. Singleton, MD, MPH
Author, *The Lyme Disease Solution*

Introduction

In October 2009, I decided to make a major, permanent change in my diet. After many years of misdiagnoses, I had finally been properly diagnosed with, and begun treatment for, Lyme disease and two other tick-borne diseases.

As most Lyme disease sufferers know, the levels of frustration with this illness are many. There seem to be no clear-cut answers as to how long a treatment might take, or which treatment will work best. Most frustrating is the lack of understanding surrounding Lyme disease and the co-infections, not just among the general population, but also in the medical community. As I go through the treatment process, it continues to be clear to me that Lyme treatment needs to be personalized for each patient, depending on which infections the patient has, how long they have been sick, how strong their immune system is and how their body reacts to certain medications, among other factors.

This lack of clear-cut solutions sent me on a quest to learn as much as I could about these illnesses. I wanted to be sure I was on the right path, that I was doing everything possible to help my body heal in conjunction with medical treatment.

Among the informative books I read was Dr. Kenneth Singletons' book, *The Lyme Disease Solution*. I found his book especially refreshing because, not only is Dr. Singleton a Lyme-literate medical doctor, but he actually had Lyme Disease himself and is now recovered. His book reassured me that I was on the right track with the treatment plan prescribed by my own Lyme specialist, but Dr. Singleton's view on nutrition and its relationship to healing was new to me.

In comparison to how many people eat, I'd always thought my diet was very healthy, and for the most part, it was. After reading Dr. Singleton's book, however, I realized I could do more. For example, based on this new information, I suspected I had sensitivities to some of the foods I'd been regularly eating. Also, I had not been eating organically grown food.

I wanted to try The Lyme Inflammation Diet® (LID) presented in the book. At first glance, I was hesitant: the initial week-long Phase is quite restrictive, because it is designed to jumpstart the body's detoxification process. I was accustomed to a dairy- and carbohydrate-rich diet, and these food groups were not permitted until Phase 3, making me wonder if I could make it through the first two Phases.

I decided to call my mother, Gail, for some help. She is a professional home economist, with a very impressive resume, but more importantly, she's the most creative and accomplished cook I've ever known. I told her my concerns, and she asked me to email her the list of foods allowed in the first Phase. Shortly after receiving the list, she called to say that there was PLENTY I could eat, and she would come up with some recipes for me. By the end of the day, I had received several delicious-looking recipes. I started to think following the LID was not going to be nearly as challenging as I'd feared.

After following the diet for only a few days, I came up with a great idea! In addition to developing recipes, my mom is a very talented food stylist who's worked in the industry for over 35 years. And I make my living as a graphic designer and photographer. Together, we could use our skills to create a cookbook filled with beautiful, delicious and nutritious meals for the LID diet. My mom loved the idea, and with her encouragement I wrote Dr. Singleton to see if he had ever considered publishing a cookbook specific to the LID.

A few weeks later, it was to my great joy that he called and said that he and his wife, who is a nutritionist, had been considering the exact same idea, even before receiving my letter. Many excited conversations followed, and the eventual outcome was the book you now hold, *Recipes for Repair: A Lyme Disease Cookbook*.

The months spent researching the book, working with my mom, eating all of the amazing meals she created, and getting to know Dr. Singleton have been a blessing to me. I've learned so much about nutrition and the importance of a good diet. I now realize that the decisions I make about what to put into my body directly affect how I feel, and this knowledge has empowered me to take an active role in my own treatment plan.

It has been a challenge to change the habits of a diet that I'd become so accustomed to, but I've experienced first-hand the difference my food choices make in my healing process, and it was a challenge worth meeting. I now nourish my body by eating a whole foods diet, high in fresh organic vegetables, fruits, nuts and seeds and organic fish, meat and poultry, and low in carbohydrates, and I have eliminated nutrient-deficient processed food.

In the upcoming pages, you will find recipes created from all-natural, whole foods, none of which contain refined flours, pure cane sugar or any artificial ingredients. This healthy way of eating is not just for people who have health challenges like Lyme disease, but for the general population as well.

Recipes that taste "good enough" are never good enough for my mom. She feels it's bad enough that you might not be feeling well; changing the way you eat should make you feel better, not deprived. Who wants meals that taste like "diet food"?

On several occasions, I sat down to dinner with my husband, and after eating a few bites of our meal, he said, "This is really good! I hope it's in the book." That's the type of reaction my mom looked for from all her testers, especially those without any dietary restrictions. It was her hope to create a book full of recipes that taste great and that you can serve to family and friends without disclaimer. I've cooked and eaten every recipe she wrote at least once, and they're all delicious – and I have very high standards, since the best cook I've ever known prepared my meals most of my life!

We hope that the information in this book, and the 150-plus recipes you have to choose from during the weeks and months to come, will enable you to realize not only the importance of implementing The Lyme Inflammation Diet®, but also that changing your eating habits is an achievable goal – one that can be filled with many wonderful meals.

Laura Piazza, co-author
Recipes for Repair: A Lyme Disease Cookbook

Part I

Living the Lyme Inflammation Diet®

The Lyme Inflammation Diet® (LID) is based on the premise that the food you eat can help you avoid or reduce the symptoms typical of Lyme disease, while at the same time improving your overall health and strengthening your immune system to help your body eliminate the infecting bacteria.

The LID focuses primarily on managing chronic inflammation, but it also addresses toxins and out-of-balance enzymes, which are all problems typically experienced by patients with Lyme disease and other tick-borne diseases.

In this chapter, we review the mechanisms and causes of these problems and explain how the LID can help you fight them.

Understanding Chronic Inflammation

Inflammation is a natural part of your immune system's healing process. Marked by increased blood flow, swelling, redness and warmth, inflammation helps contain harmful irritants or isolate an injury, while also rushing healing agents to the afflicted area.

At times, however, inflammation gets out of control – your immune system thinks your body is under continuous attack – and this can lead to an abnormal, long-lasting state called *chronic inflammation*.

Chronic inflammation is a cause of many symptoms associated with Lyme disease, other tick-borne diseases and other afflictions: joint and muscle pain, swelling, stiffness, indigestion, congestion, diarrhea, breathing difficulties, weight gain and more. The bacterium responsible for Lyme disease – *Borrelia burgdorferi* or Bb – causes inflammation, but so do many other health and environmental factors. Most notably, the Standard American Diet (known, too appropriately, as SAD) is notorious for causing and exacerbating inflammation.

In this section, we look at how chronic inflammation works and the factors that cause it, in preparation for understanding how improving your diet can be an effective anti-inflammation strategy.

The Mechanisms of Chronic Inflammation

Inflammation is a normal bodily process triggered by your immune system in response to injury, infection, allergens, temporary stress or other damaging factors. In healthy people, the inflammation process is *acute*: short-lived, and ending when the original problem is resolved. When inflammation becomes chronic, however, a wide range of health problems can eventually arise.

To better understand why chronic inflammation is so hazardous, let's look at what happens inside your body when inflammation becomes chronic.

At the beginning of an acute inflammation response, your immune system rapidly releases specific hormones, proteins and other chemicals that act in unison to dilate your blood vessels. This increases blood flow and swells tissue in the area the immune system is attempting to heal. The immune system then unleashes a second wave of chemicals – cytokines, eosinophils, prostaglandins, leukotrines and interleukins – that continue the inflammation process, resulting in further tissue swelling, redness and possibly sensations of heat and pain.

The body then makes proteins called *antibodies* that seek out and attach to the invaders, which are called antigens. When the antibodies and the antigens come together in battle, they form what are called *circulating immune complexes* (CICs).

Good CICs occur when there are enough antibodies to exceed and overwhelm the antigens. This type of CIC causes a chemical reaction that enables the white blood cells to eat (or phagocytize) the foreigners. The CICs are then cleared away in the bloodstream, and inflammation is kept to a minimum.

Bad CICs occur when there aren't enough antibodies to overwhelm the invaders, and the CICs contain more antigen than antibody. When this happens, the CICs become deposited in tissue instead of being cleared by the white blood cells, resulting in inflammation.

Chronic inflammation can be caused by an unresolved acute inflammatory response like the one just described, or it may develop on its own (encouraged by several factors described below). In either case, the immune system believes the body is still under attack, and tries to continue its healing functions. This action is appropriate in the case of infections like Lyme disease – the body *is* still under attack! But in other cases, including in some people with properly monitored and treated Lyme disease, the perception of attack by the immune system is faulty. The result is that the immune system literally starts to attack the wrong parts of the body, such as joints, organs and other tissues. This inappropriate activity on the part of the immune system is known as *autoimmune dysfunction*, an increasingly common cause of chronic inflammation in many people today.

Chronic Inflammation and Lyme Disease

Lyme disease and chronic inflammation are a terrible combination, and the degree to which chronic low-grade inflammation exists in the body is directly related to the severity of symptoms that Lyme patients experience.

Lyme disease itself can trigger chronic inflammation, and any inflammation that exists before infection impairs the immune system's ability to fight off the invading bacteria. The cycle of infection and increasing inflammation gives the bacteria an ever-stronger foothold in the body, causing increasingly severe health symptoms. This relationship between chronic inflammation and Lyme disease explains why the severity of symptoms for people with widespread Lyme disease can vary so greatly, with some people nearly incapacitated and others only mildly affected.

Fortunately, following the LID should, over time, produce powerful anti-inflammatory effects. The reduction in inflammation will in turn reduce the burden on your body's immune system and other organ systems, so that it can more effectively target and eliminate Bb bacteria and other co-infections.

The Causes of Chronic Inflammation

Medical science recognizes several specific potential causes of unhealthy inflammation. Most of these are rooted in or exacerbated by poor diet, and the LID can help you avoid or overcome them. Let's review these various causes before getting into the LID.

- **Infectious Microorganisms.** Bacteria (including Bb and the various tick-borne co-infection bacterium), mold, fungi, parasites and viruses all initiate an inflammation response that can become chronic if the offenders can't be eliminated. Some organisms even disrupt the body's normal inflammation control mechanisms for their own protection; for example, the Bb induces the manufacture of IL-10 to suppress the immune system's Th1 response (see Chapter 4 of *The Lyme Disease Solution* for more information).

- **Allergies and Sensitivities.** Though the terms are often used interchangeably, allergy and sensitivity are actually caused by quite different immune mechanisms. An example of a food allergy is peanut allergy, which causes an immediate, severe, often life-threatening reaction. An example of a food sensitivity is celiac disease, in which a non-allergic immune reaction occurs in response to gluten, resulting in chronic inflammation as long as the person keeps eating foods containing gluten. Most chronic inflammation triggers are sensitivities rather than allergies: because exposure to the sensitizing substance is persistent, the immune system doesn't shut down the normal inflammation process. The sensitizing substances that can trigger an immune response include environmental materials such as chemicals, pollutants and toxins, and foods and food products.

- **Environmental Toxins and Pollutants.** When toxins and pollutants become lodged in the body, the immune system struggles to eliminate them, resulting in chronic inflammation. Toxic environmental chemicals can cause a variety of additional health problems, including cancer, that also throw off the immune system. We'll return to look more at toxins in a later section.

- **Cigarette Smoking.** Smoking is a significant cause of chronic inflammation and reduced immune function. Also, bacteria don't like oxygen, and so smoking deprives the body of one of its most useful tools to fight Lyme: oxygen. Lyme patients who stop smoking have a much better outcome than those who do not. If you smoke, seek help in quitting.

- **Free Radical Damage.** Free radicals are unstable atom groups that occur naturally as part of the body's oxidation process. They are normally balanced by the presence of antioxidants, which act to neutralize them. When this process fails, the unchecked free radicals circulate throughout the body, damage cells, and lead to chronic inflammation. An unbalanced diet low in foods containing antioxidants (fruits and vegetables) and high in foods that contribute to excessive oxidation (processed and fried foods) is therefore a major contributor to chronic inflammation.

- **Obesity.** Chronic inflammation is often a problem for people who are overweight because fat cells may release chemical substances (*cytokines*) that can cause inflammation. Many obese people also suffer from two other significant contributors to chronic inflammation: insulin resistance and leptin resistance.

- **Insulin Resistance.** Insulin is a hormone produced by the pancreas to help pass glucose from the bloodstream, where it circulates to the cells that need it to function. Glucose is a type of sugar that acts as the body's chief fuel; its primary source is carbohydrates in our diet. Insulin resistance occurs when the amount of insulin produced by the pancreas is too small to enable glucose to pass into the cells. Glucose then builds up in the blood, and the pancreas tries to produce even more insulin to balance the glucose level. This imbalance can result in high blood sugar (hyperglycemia) or type 2 diabetes, and can also encourage chronic inflammation. Chronic inflammation itself can also cause insulin resistance, resulting in a vicious cycle of unhealthy consequences.

- **Leptin Resistance.** Leptins belong to a special class of hormones known as *adipokines* that are produced by your body's fat cells. Leptins help the brain know how much body fat you have, helping to reduce appetite and increase metabolism so you don't become overweight. In women, leptins also help regulate fertility and the functioning of the ovaries. Leptin resistance occurs when leptins no longer perform their job properly. The problem isn't that the leptins are malfunctioning, but that the fat cells aren't properly responding to the messages the leptins are sending them. This causes the body to produce even more leptins, which in turn can contribute to chronic inflammation. As with insulin resistance, chronic inflammation can also cause leptin resistance, setting up another vicious cycle of unhealthy conditions in the body.

- **Advanced Glycation End Products (AGEs).** These unstable, toxic compounds form when excessive simple sugars abnormally bind to proteins. The body mounts an immune attack against the resulting "foreign" AGEs, resulting in inflammation. AGEs have been associated with several diseases linked to chronic inflammation, including Alzheimer's disease, arthritis, atherosclerosis (hardening of the arteries), diabetes, high blood pressure and certain types of vision problems including cataracts and macular degeneration.

  There are two sources of AGEs. *Exogenous* AGEs are already present in food we eat, especially in poor-quality carbohydrates (such as cakes and donuts) and fried or high-temperature-cooked foods (such as barbecued meats). *Endogenous* AGEs are created in the body after we ingest certain foods, usually after the excessive use of sugar (such as sucrose and glucose) and fructose (such as high fructose corn syrup). Either way, AGEs contribute to inflammation, and their primary source is a poor diet of unhealthy carbohydrates, sugar and overcooked foods.

- **Fatigue and Lack of Sleep.** Failing to get at least seven or more hours of sleep on a regular basis can lead to persistent or chronic fatigue. This in turn causes stress and low energy levels, which can contribute to chronic inflammation. Sleep disruption may also alter the endorphin cycle and hinder proper adrenal function, both important bodily processes for controlling inflammation.

- **Lack of Regular Exercise.** Among its many health benefits, exercise helps to reduce stress. Conversely, lack of exercise can contribute to stress buildup, thereby leading to chronic inflammation. Additionally, exercise strengthens and regulates the immune system – and its ability to regulate inflammation – by increasing the body's normal production of endorphins.

- **Poor Diet.** Perhaps the most widespread and serious cause of chronic inflammation is eating foods that either encourage chronic inflammation, or don't encourage a healthy body and immune system, or both.

The standard diet of most people in the United States is excessive in processed fast foods and other nutrient-deficient food products, and is the number one lifestyle choice responsible for our nation's healthcare crisis. It's a primary source of free radicals, food allergens, oxidized fats (from fried foods), excessive omega-6 fatty acids (and deficient omega-3s), empty calories, sugar, AGEs and many, many other unhealthy ingredients. All of these potentially harmful products can cause or prolong chronic inflammation.

By taking responsibility for your diet and following the guidelines of the LID, there is much you can do to significantly reduce and eventually eliminate chronic inflammation. We believe that taking this step is absolutely essential in helping your body more effectively cope with and reverse Lyme disease, co-infections and the resulting chronic inflammation.

Assessing Your Risk for Chronic Inflammation
A simple and inexpensive blood test, the CRP, can help your physician determine whether or not you suffer from chronic inflammation, and the extent of the problem.

CRP stands for C-reactive protein, a type of protein that is present in small amounts in the blood of all people. As chronic inflammation sets in, levels of CRP in the bloodstream become elevated because the liver produces more C-reactive protein in response to the inflammation. Ask your doctor about the CRP test, which is widely available across the country.

In addition to the blood test, the LID Self-Assessment Tool (see pages 30-31) covers many factors that can improve or worsen inflammation, and can help you quickly determine your chronic inflammation risk level. If your answers indicate a high level of inflammation risk, the good news is that you can reverse all of the lifestyle risk factors, adding to the benefits of the LID.

Chronic Inflammation Self-Assessment Tool

Positive (Anti-Inflammatory) Daily Dietary and Lifestyle Factors

Award yourself the indicated positive (+) number for each of the following items that are part of your average daily or weekly dietary and lifestyle routine. If the item does not apply to you, leave that particular score blank.

___ *Fruit Consumption*
(5 points for each serving of fresh, frozen or dried organic fruit you consume per day; 3 points for each serving of unsweetened fruit juice)

___ *Vegetable Consumption*
(5 points for each serving of raw or steamed vegetables)

___ *Daily Vitamin/Mineral/Antioxidant Supplementation*
(5 points)

___ *Consumption of Oily Fish (e.g., Salmon) or Omega-3/Fish Oil Supplements*
(7 points for consumption four or more times/week; 4 points for consumption 1-3 times/week)

___ *Organic or Range-Fed Meat Consumption*
(5 points)

___ *Regular Use of Olive Oil and/or Other Healthy Oils for Cooking*
(5 points)

___ *Regular Exercise*
(3 points for each 10 minutes of exercise performed per day)

___ *Consumption of Pure, Filtered Water*
(1 point for each 8-ounce glass of water; 8 points total for 8 glasses or more)

___ *Laughter*
(2 points for each good, hearty laugh per day, up to 6 points total)

___ *Positive Attitude/Gratefulness/Giving Spirit*
(7 points)

___ *Daily Prayer or Meditation*
(7 points)

___ *Daily Exposure to Sunlight for 10 or More Minutes*
(5 points)

___ *Daily Exposure to Fresh Air/Deep Breathing Exercises*
(4 points)

___ *Healthy Relationships and Social Networks*
(5 points for each, including church groups, therapy and so forth)

___ *Daily Giving and Receiving Hugs*
(2 points for each hug, up to 6 points total)

[ ] *Total Positive Score:* (add all the above scores)

Negative (Pro-Inflammatory) Daily Dietary and Lifestyle Factors
Give yourself the indicated negative (-) number (e.g., -5) for each of the following items that are part of your regular dietary and lifestyle routine. If the item does not apply to you, leave that particular score blank.

___ *Smoking*
(-10 points for each pack smoked)

___ *Overweight*
(-7 points if up to 50 pounds overweight; -10 points if over 50 pounds overweight)

___ *Consumption of Wheat, Dairy or other Sensitivity-Causing Foods*
(- 5 points for each food consumed daily – e.g., eating bread daily = -5))

___ *Use of Trans-Fatty Acids (margarine, hydrogenated and partially-hydrogenated oils)*
(-5 points for each time used per day)

___ *Exposure to External AGEs (fried foods, doughnuts, pastries, etc.)*
(-5 points for each exposure per day)

___ *Consumption of Sugar or Artificial Sweeteners (aspartame, splenda, etc.)*
(- 5 points for each food consumed daily – e.g., eating bread daily = -5)

___ *Excess Omega-6 Fatty Acid (Arachidonic Acid) Consumption (including corn and other vegetable oils)*
(-3 points for each time consumed per day)

___ *Use of Cooking Oils Other than Olive or Other Healthy Oils*
(-5 points)

___ *Alcohol*
(-7 points for each alcoholic beverage consumed per day)

___ *Negative/Pessimistic Attitude and/or Victim Mentality*
(-7 points)

___ *Tendency Towards Unforgiveness*
(-7 points)

___ *Averaging Less Than Seven Hours of Sleep*
(-7 points)

___ *Poor Water Intake*
(-7 points for less than six 8-ounce glasses per day)

___ *Chronic Exposure to Mold in Home or at Work*
(-5 points)

___ *Less than Ten Minutes of Daily Sun Exposure*
(- 4 points)

☐ *Total Negative Score* (add all the <u>above</u> scores)

☐ *Combine both of your positive and negative scores to tally your NET SCORE.*

Rating

50 or above = Excellent (Very low risk of chronic inflammation)
25 to 49 = Very Good
0 to 24 = Fair

-1 to -24 = Poor
-25 to -49 = Very Bad
-50 or below = Emergency (Extremely high risk of chronic inflammation)

About Toxins and Enzymes

While the primary focus of the LID is controlling inflammation, it also has the related goals of reducing toxins in your body and helping your enzymes stay in balance.

Toxins and the Need for Detoxification

Our daily environment and our typically poor diet expose our bodies to an alarming amount of toxins. When the organs of detoxification, such as the liver and skin, are unable to keep up with this toxic assault, toxins become lodged in the cells. Tissues – particularly fat cells and tissues – then start to wreak havoc on a variety of body processes.

This can result in impaired immune function, impaired metabolism, hormonal imbalances, increased inflammation, diminished cognitive function, chronic lack of energy, unhealthy weight gain and many other health problems.

Of particular significance to people infected with Bb and other tick-borne infections is the role that toxins can play in helping these harmful microorganisms escape elimination. Research indicates that toxins make it more difficult for the immune system to identify and target harmful bacteria, fungi and viruses, making it easier for such microorganisms to take deeper root in the body and cause more serious symptoms. Lessening the body's toxic burden is therefore vitally important in all cases of chronic infection. As we shall see in a later section, the LID can help.

Enzymes and Their Role

Systemic enzymes are one of the most fascinating natural therapies for treating chronic inflammation.

An enzyme is a type of protein that facilitates a chemical reaction that in turn causes change to another substance. Digestive enzymes are one good example: when you chew, enzymes in your mouth begin breaking down carbohydrates so they can be absorbed when arriving in the intestines. Other enzymes (from the pancreas, primarily) join the mouth enzymes in the intestines to further break down carbohydrates and other food elements such as proteins and fats. Without these enzymes, your food would never be broken into absorbable components, and malnutrition would result. (See *The Lyme Disease Solution* for more on the complex interplay of Lyme disease, enzymes and chronic inflammation.)

We produce hundreds of different types of enzymes in our bodies, each with specific purposes and functions. Even so, it's also essential that we ingest additional enzymes in our foods. The problem is that many of the best sources of food enzymes (such as fruits and vegetables) are typically overly processed or overcooked and so have lost significant amounts of their enzyme content. Additionally, chronic illness increases the body's requirements for enzymes. This combination of illness and typically inadequate diet sets up Lyme disease patients for one of the worst consequences of enzyme deficiency: chronic inflammation.

Fortunately, the LID is a "high enzyme" nutrition program, which is one of the reasons for its effectiveness.

The Lyme Inflammation Diet®

While stress management, regular exercise, healthy eating and proper sleep are all vitally important to a healthy immune system, probably the single most important step you can take to prevent and reverse chronic inflammation is to commit to a healthy diet.

Such a diet should ideally consist entirely of foods and beverages that don't trigger the inflammation response, and that contribute to detoxification and enzyme balance. Dr. Singleton's Lyme Inflammation Diet® defines a protocol and specifies foods to help you come as close as possible to this ideal.

The LID is powerfully effective, and following it can help to reverse chronic inflammation and boost your immune system's ability to fight Bb bacteria and other infectious microorganisms. In addition, this nutrition program will help significantly reduce or eliminate both insulin resistance and leptin resistance. The dietary recommendations will further help you build a foundation of wellness by supplying your body with a rich supply of nutrients, including the fiber, vitamins, minerals, antioxidants, essential fats and other vital substances that it needs in order to function optimally.

Phases of the LID

The LID approach instructs you in first eliminating the most common food contributors to chronic inflammation, then gradually adding back foods and monitoring the effects to establish a broad yet healthy diet. The diet has four Phases; once a food is introduced, you may continue to use it in each subsequent Phase.

Phase 1: Induction. The goal of the first Phase is to shut down the mechanisms of chronic inflammation in your body while also performing detoxification. It's probably the toughest of the four Phases, but it only lasts a week. Food is very restricted during this Phase (see page 70-71).

Phase 2: Early Reentry. The second Phase begins the process of relaxing food restrictions to see how you are affected. Phase 2 permits additional new items in each food group (see pages 108-109), which you should add back into your meals very slowly, over the course of at least three weeks. If any new food seems to aggravate your inflammation symptoms, stop using it until later, after your body heals a bit more.

Phase 3: Late Reentry. Once confident that the Phase 2 foods are safe, you may begin Phase 3, which introduces foods generally considered healthy, but

---

Ed's LID Experience

Below is the story of Ed, one of Dr. Singleton's patients, as told in The Lyme Disease Solution.

Ed came to our office after suffering from severe Lyme arthritic symptoms for several years.

A hard-working man, Ed woke for work at 4:00 a.m. every morning, and stopped at the corner fast-food store for his coffee, donut or pastry, and sometimes fried tater tots. At lunch he would usually have a diet cola (extra large), along with two hot dogs on white buns smothered with pickles, mayonnaise, ketchup and mustard, and an order of French fries on the side. For dinner, his wife would prepare potatoes and steak, along with one vegetable and several dinner rolls, and ice cream for dessert. While watching TV in the evening, Ed would usually have two or three beers and nachos with cheese dip or guacamole.

As Ed described his diet, I was shocked by several things: the complete lack of fruit, the nearly complete lack of fiber, the relative lack of vegetables, the excess of sugar and fried foods and, finally, the use of coffee, colas and beer instead of water.

I told Ed he would have to make major changes in his dietary program if he wanted to get well. I explained that

if he was willing to follow the Lyme Inflammation Diet®, he would feel significantly better by the time of his one-month follow-up visit, and that we would begin antibiotics at that time.

Ed's wife, sitting beside him, smiled and said her husband could never follow this radical approach to diet. Ed, however, is the kind of man who loves a challenge: he said he would do it, and he did.

One month later, Ed returned with the good news that his joints were 75% better, his energy was 50% better, and his thinking processes were also 50% better. His wife added that he also wasn't as grouchy as usual. Remember, these improvements all happened before we started Ed on antibiotics. They happened because the Lyme Inflammation Diet® not only greatly reduced Ed's inflammation, but also supplied the necessary antioxidants and vital nutrients his body had been craving for years.

Ed's positive experience with adopting the LID has been quite common among the many patients I have treated for Lyme disease.

known to cause inflammation in some people (see pages 154-155). You must again introduce each new food item slowly and deliberately over at least a four-week period, monitoring yourself for inflammation effects and adjusting accordingly.

Phase 4: Maintenance. If all has gone well, you can initiate Phase 4 just eight weeks after first starting Phase 1. Phase 4 allows you to introduce even more healthy foods – again, slowly and with careful monitoring – and to reach a maintenance level where you have a wide variety of healthy food options and little or no symptoms of chronic inflammation (see page 207).

In addition to the specifics of each LID Phase, there are several fundamental food and diet guidelines you should always observe, as described in the next section.

General Food Guidelines

Follow these guidelines during and after all four Phases of the LID to maintain the health benefits you've achieved.

As you become more conscious of the relationship between healthy eating and good health, pay attention to how the foods you eat make you feel. You'll notice a big difference between the physical and emotional satisfaction derived from high-quality, nutrient-dense foods, and the addictive "quick fix" feelings that come from eating unhealthy foods. By tuning into how you feel as you eat, you'll develop an unerring instinct for what foods are most appropriate for you, and when you should eat them.

Generally, the foods you eat each day should consist of a wide array of fresh vegetables (preferably organic), high-quality protein foods, whole grains and quality fats. All should be eaten as close to their natural state as possible, which means no fast foods or processed and refined foods.

- Avoid sodas and all commercial beverages, including carbonated beverages that contain sugar or artificial sweeteners, sports drinks with added sugar, commercial fruit and vegetable juices and any beverage that contains salt, sweeteners and/or other chemical additives and preservatives.

- Avoid all commercially-packaged foods.

- Avoid all fried foods.

- Eat fresh fruits rather than canned, and limit your intake of fruits that are high in natural sugar content, such as bananas, grapes and raisins.

- Avoid the use of all refined carbohydrates, including white pasta, white rice, white flour and white flour products.

- Avoid sugary desserts, especially cakes, donuts, pastries and other cooked high-sugar products that are high in exogenous AGEs.

- Avoid honey-glazed meats, barbecued meats and processed commercial meat products. This includes bacon, bologna, hot dogs, salami and sausage, as well as all fast-food fish, meats and poultry.

- Avoid all shellfish, farm-raised fish and non-organic beef, chicken, lamb and turkey. Eat pork only occasionally.

- Avoid all trans-fatty acids and hydrogenated and partially hydrogenated oils, as well as lard, margarine and shortenings. Avoid vegetable oils, such as corn and cottonseed oil.

- Enjoy sources of good fats, including coconut and extra virgin olive oil, avocado, nuts and seeds, sesame oil, organic butter (especially from pasture-fed cows), organic raw milk cheese and other cheeses from pasture-fed cows.

- For cooking purposes, use olive oil (or olive combined with sesame oil) in general, and coconut oil for high-temperature cooking.

- Avoid the use of table salt (Celtic and sea salt are both permissible).

Dealing with Sugar Cravings

Discontinuing all use of sugar is essential for recovery from chronic inflammation. It's difficult, though, because sugar is addictive. Here are some tactics for dealing with the inevitable cravings.

Plan on feeling feel poorly for about three days while your body adjusts to the sudden lack of sugar.

Eat multiple small meals each day, making sure to include a source of protein and quality fat at each meal. Almonds are a good snack; they contain healthy protein and fat.

Take a good quality multi-vitamin that contains B-complex and chromium.

Always consult a physician before adding supplements as they may interfere or have adverse effects in combination with any prescriptions you are taking. If your healthcare provider approves them for you, three supplements that might help are glutamine, alpha lipoic acid and 5-hydroxytryptophan.

Your cravings for sugar should be greatly reduced by about one month after quitting it. Sugar will then seem extremely sweet, and you'll feel lousy when you eat it (especially on an empty stomach). You'll also notice increased energy and weight loss, and your gastrointestinal system will work better.

- Avoid all food additives, especially aspartame, MSG, nitrates and sulfites.

- Be sure to have a healthy breakfast. Many health experts consider breakfast the most important meal of the day, so don't skip it!

- Avoid alcohol completely during Lyme treatment and for at least three to six months after you stop taking antibiotics. While it's best that you abstain permanently, if you do choose to drink alcohol, limit yourself to one to two glasses of wine (or one to two beers) per day, after you complete the three to six month abstinence period.

Food Choices and Detoxification

If your healthcare practitioner determines that your body is particularly suffering from toxins of any sort, there are some additional factors you should keep in mind while undertaking the LID.

As with all health issues, prevention is key when it comes to dealing with toxins. Wise food choices can also support your liver in its role of cleansing the body of Lyme toxins and antibiotic residue.

- Concentrate your LID choices on "brain foods," including water, egg yolks, raw organic peanuts and other nuts, wheat germ, liver, meat, fish, cruciferous vegetables, beans, turkey, milk, potatoes, whole grains, antioxidant fruits, avocado and other healthy omega-3 and -6 foods and green vegetables.

- Make foods high in omega-3 oils a regular part of your diet. Sardines and wild-caught salmon are excellent food choices for this purpose.

- Eat plenty of raw foods, especially fresh fruits and vegetables. Plant-based foods (except for beans, potatoes and tomatoes) help the processes of liver detoxification more when consumed raw or juiced, rather than cooked. Artichokes and dandelion leaves are two notable liver-helpful vegetables, and these fruits and vegetables are also particularly helpful: apples, blueberries, cherries, grapes, lemons, pineapple, beet greens, celery, garlic, green leafy vegetables and onions.

- Eat only organic foods, if possible. Non-organic foods contain herbicides, pesticides and other substances that add to the burden of liver detoxification. Organic foods, by contrast, help to reduce the toxin burden placed on the liver.

- Glutathione is considered a "superfood" when it comes to detoxification and antioxidant properties. Foods with sulphur-rich amino acids can increase your Glutathione level; such foods include asparagus, broccoli, avocado, spinach, raw eggs, garlic and fresh unprocessed meats.

- The Indian spice curcumin (turmeric) has been found to help by increasing the expression of glutathione S-transferase and protecting neurons exposed to oxidant-stressing brain cells called astrocytes.

- Vitamin C aids in the overall process of detoxification and provides many other health benefits, including improved immunity. Vitamin C and niacin (vitamin B3) both help fat cells and tissues expel toxins (but may cause severe flushing).

- Garlic aids detoxification and also has antimicrobial characteristics.

Probiotics Balance Antibiotics

Patients using antibiotics – as is typical for Lyme disease – must be concerned about balancing the negative effects of those drugs with the healthful benefits of probiotics.

Antibiotics can destroy the intestinal tract bacteria responsible for food digestion. Probiotics introduce new healthy bacteria to your system. It's normally sufficient to consume foods that are good natural sources of probiotics (fermented foods such as kefir, yogurt, kombucha, tempeh and sauerkraut are especially good sources). When taking antibiotics, however, it's generally best to supplement your diet with a high quality probiotic formula on a daily basis.

Be sure to carefully time and sequence your daily antibiotic and probiotic doses. If you take them together, they'll in effect cancel each other out. Generally, a separation of two or more hours ensures that both work effectively.

Also, note that it is important to continue taking probiotics for several weeks (and sometimes months) after antibiotics have been discontinued to fully restore the normal balance of intestinal bacteria.

Consult your healthcare provider for information and recommendations on the best use of probiotics in your particular case.

- Cilantro is another powerful herb; it acts as a natural detoxifying "magnet" that pulls toxins from the body (including heavy metals). If you enjoy the flavor of cilantro, add it to your meals to aid in detoxification, especially in the early Phases of the LID.

- Make nuts a regular part of your diet, as they assist both liver and gallbladder function. They are an excellent source of healthy oils and quality protein, and thus make an ideal snack food between meals.

- Finally, drinking plenty of pure, filtered water every day is one of the simplest and most effective steps you can take to reduce toxins in your body. (For further tips on preventing toxic buildup in your body, see pages 391-400 of *The Lyme Disease Solution*.)

Special Dietary Considerations for Problem Headaches

Most people suffer from occasional headaches that are easily relieved by simple measures, such as rest or acetaminophen. If you suffer from chronic or frequent headaches, food sensitivities could be playing a significant role. An offending food can cause headaches by triggering changes to the blood vessels in the head, with or without the presence of other inflammation in the body. Migraines are an example of this kind of headache.

Identifying which foods are the culprits is difficult. Here are five steps you can take in the process of elimination.

1. **Avoid additives and artificial sweeteners.** Many foods contain artificial flavors, colors or sweeteners that can alter the blood flow to the brain and trigger a nasty headache. An especially common culprit is the artificial sweetener aspartame, which can even cause neurological problems. The foods recommended for the LID are all additive-free.

2. **Consider tyramine elimination.** Tyramine is a common, natural substance formed from the breakdown of protein as food ages. Generally speaking, the longer a high-protein food ages, the greater its tyramine content. Common signs of tyramine sensitivity include: acute and often severe headache, increase in blood pressure, anxiety, depression, tiredness, heart palpitations, nausea, vomiting or dizziness. Tyramine-containing foods are minimized or avoided in the LID. Such foods include aged cheeses, yogurt, alcoholic beverages, bananas, prunes, raisins, ripe avocado, pineapple, vanilla, broad beans, eggplant, snow peas, lentils, most nuts, chocolate, soy sauce, Chinese vegetables, pickled herring, canned meats, sausages and preserved meats and brewer's yeast. Aged cheeses have the highest levels, and the toxic effect of tyramine is sometimes called "the cheese effect."

3. **Beware of caffeine.** Widely used in coffee, tea, chocolate, soft drinks and even some medications, regular consumption of caffeine can lead to dependency, and withdrawal from it can cause severe headaches. Consider avoiding caffeine completely, or limiting its use (such as only drinking it in green tea).

4. **Watch out for MSG.** Monosodium glutamate is a flavoring additive found in many Asian foods that's commonly linked to headaches and migraines. No LID foods contain MSG. When dining out, request that your meal be prepared without MSG.

5. **Go alcohol-free.** As mentioned repeatedly throughout this book, you should avoid alcohol when recovering from inflammation or other health problems. In addition to containing tyramine, alcohol increases blood flow to the brain – which can cause headaches – and certain alcohols have other components that may induce headaches, such as the nitrates found in wine.

Refined Foods: Progress or Setback?

Over one hundred years ago, preparing a meal was a much more complex task than it is today. Meals depended on hunting, fishing and farming. Cooking involved preparation of foods that were bought locally and fresh, or that came from your own land. While this type of food preparation may be inconvenient or impossible in our fast-paced, busy lives, food in those days was fresh and as close to the original food source as possible, and thus was filled with the nutrients our bodies need.

In the late 1800s, new technology for grinding flour was invented. No longer did whole grains need to be ground by the tedious process of stone grinding. Grains could now be ground using iron, steel or porcelain rollers, which produced a much finer, whiter flour, but which also stripped nutrients away from the original grain.

This new, finely ground flour no longer attracted insects, bacteria or rodents, which might seem like a benefit, except that what had attracted them in the first place were the nutrients that were now missing. Additionally, the new flour lasted months on the shelves and was much easier to transport, a positive change. Eventually, though, people became deficient in certain vitamins because the vitamins had been removed from the whole grains. With current technology, this is no longer a problem, as flours can be enriched with the missing vitamins and minerals.

This was the start of a new modern diet. It truly is a convenient way of eating. We can have a fully prepared meal (from the freezer section) in a matter of minutes. And our food can last months or years in our cupboards. But at what cost?

The modern diet is high in refined fats and sugars and lacking in whole grains, and it contains artificial ingredients. Our bodies are not getting the nutrients they require, and we are consuming ingredients that are artificial, sometimes useless and sometimes harmful.

As you'll learn in this book, eating and preparing the freshest foods that do not contain refined ingredients can do wonders for your health. In the pages to come, it is our hope that you realize that eating fresh, unrefined whole foods is not as overwhelming as it might seem.

Organic Versus Conventional

In 1990, the U.S. Congress first adopted the Organic Foods Production Act (OFPA) as part of the 1990 Farm Bill. Since that time, the criteria for products sold under the organic label have undergone extensive debate and public input, resulting in a stringent set of official standards adopted by the USDA's National Organic Program, first published in December 2000, and implemented in October 2002. These national organic standards require that specific practices be observed in the production and processing of agricultural ingredients certified as organic. The standards apply to the methods, practices and substances used in producing and handling crops, livestock and processed agricultural products, and they are strictly enforced. Organic growers and handlers must be certified by the USDA, and anyone who knowingly labels or sells an unqualified product as organic can be subject to a civil penalty of up to $10,000 per violation.

What Does "Organic" Really Mean?

Below are seven good reasons to buy organic food, excerpted from the Northeast Organic Farming Association of New Hampshire's "Why Buy Organic?" brochure. Visit www.nofanh.org/whybuyorganic to read the brochure in its entirety.

No persistent chemicals. Instead of using chemical fertilizers, herbicides, or fungicides that are often highly toxic, persist in the environment, and leach into soil and groundwater, organic standards require a program of soil building that protects against soil erosion and water pollution.

No synthetic pesticides. Organic standards prohibit the use of synthetic pesticides. No amount of scrubbing will remove pesticides that have been absorbed into a crop.

No genetic engineering. Organic standards prohibit the use of genetically modified organisms (GMOs) for seed or stock. Until compulsory GMO labeling is adopted in this country, buying certified 100% organic products is the best way to keep genetic engineering out of your food.

No antibiotics. Organic standards prohibit routine use of antibiotics in livestock operations. US government regulations permit conventionally-raised animals to be regularly fed subtherapeutic levels of antibiotics to promote growth and prevent disease due to their overcrowded conditions.

No growth hormones. Organic standards prohibit the use of growth hormones, which are used in conventional livestock operations to increase the growth rate of animals or to stimulate the production of milk.

No sludge. Organic standards prohibit the use of sewage sludge as fertilizer, relying instead on the use of composted manure, crop residues, green manures, cover crops, crop rotations, companion planting, and natural mineral supplements to provide needed nutrients to plants.

No irradiation. Organic standards prohibit the use of ionizing radiation to preserve food. Proponents argue that irradiation extends shelf life by killing microbes that spoil food and cause illness. Opponents argue that it also breaks down the enzymes and vitamins that make the food healthy in the first place. They suggest cleaning up industrial feedlots and food processing operations as a better way to protect the public from E. coli and other pathogens.

Where Can I Find Organic Food?

Organic products can be found in grocery stores, cooperatives, specialty stores, farmers' markets, farm stands, online and in many restaurants.

What Should I Look For to Be Sure the Foods I Buy Are Certified Organic?

When you shop, look for the "USDA Organic" seal, or other approved labeling. Products labeled "100% Organic" and carrying the "USDA Organic" seal contain only organically produced ingredients. Products made from at least 95% organic ingredients, with the remaining ingredients approved for use in organic products, may also carry the "USDA Organic" seal. In addition, products that contain at least 70% organic ingredients may list those ingredients as organic on the packaging. Producers and processors do not have to label their foods as organic – they may use organic ingredients without being required to label them as such.

What About Unlabeled Locally Grown or Imported Foods?

At farmers' markets, it is not uncommon to see hand-written signs that say "grown without the use of pesticides" or "raised without antibiotics or growth hormones" alongside the produce and meats. While these products might not bear the official "USDA Organic" seal, that may be only because these local farmers have not applied for official organic status, which can be costly for a small farm. When buying your meat, eggs, dairy and produce at local farm stands or farmers' markets, talk to the farmer. You'll often find that the local food you're buying is meeting, or close to meeting, the organic standards.

According to the Organic Trade Association, the organic food industry is the most heavily regulated and closely monitored production system in the United States. When buying food that is imported, such as nuts or coffee, be aware that food grown in other countries is not always subject to the same standards as domestically-grown foods.

What If I Can't Afford to Buy Organic?

Unfortunately, organic food does cost more than non-organic, and eating a full diet of 100% organic food is often not financially possible. If you must choose which foods to spend the extra money on, keep the following points in mind.

For meats, fish, poultry, dairy, eggs and other animal-derived products, it is well worth spending the extra money to buy organic. Organic livestock production guidelines ensure that the livestock are fed 100% organically, and are raised without the use of antibiotics and synthetic growth hormones.

Eating only organic fruits and vegetables is quite difficult to do. Not only is it more expensive, but for some fruits and veggies, an organic option isn't even available. The following charts list the top ten fruits and vegetables that are either the most or the least likely to contain pesticides or other harmful toxins. If eating all organic produce is not an option, refer to the chart below to see which foods are the cleanest, and which most at risk for contamination.

	Fruits		Vegetables
Lowest	1 Avocado	1	Onions
	2 Pineapples	2	Sweet corn (frozen)
	3 Mango (subtropical and tropical)	3	Sweet peas (frozen)
	4 Kiwi fruit (subtropical and tropical)	4	Asparagus
	5 Cantaloupe (domestic)	5	Cabbage
	6 Watermelon	6	Eggplant
	7 Grapefruit	7	Sweet potatoes
	8 Honeydew melon	8	Winter squash
	9 Plums (domestic)	9	Broccoli
	10 Cranberries	10	Tomatoes
	1 Peaches	1	Celery
	2 Strawberries	2	Sweet bell peppers
	3 Apples	3	Spinach
	4 Blueberries (domestic)	4	Kale/collard greens
	5 Nectarines	5	Potatoes
	6 Cherries	6	Lettuce
	7 Grapes (imported)	7	Carrots
	8 Blueberries (imported)	8	Green beans (domestic)
	9 Pears	9	Summer squash
Highest	10 Plums (imported)	10	Cucumbers (imported)

Levels of pesticides and other harmful toxins (vertical axis label, from Lowest at top to Highest at bottom)

Source: www.foodnews.org (to see the full list, go to www.foodnews.org/fulllist.php)

How to Read "Nutrition Facts" Food Labels

The Nutrition Facts food label on every packaged food contains all the information you need to make an informed decision about which foods to buy. It is important that you become an avid label reader, as many packaged foods often contain sugars and other sweeteners, as well as artificial and refined ingredients, all of which should be avoided for the best possible outcome in your recovery. The secret to reading a food label is knowing what to look for.

How to Read a Nutrition Label

Important and reliable information can be found on the nutrition Nutrition Facts panel and ingredient listing. Below is a label from a can of organic tomato paste, with each section of the label defined.

A
B

Nutrition Facts
Serving Size 2 Tbsp (33g)
Servings Per Container About 5

Amount Per Serving

C **Calories** 30   Calories from Fat 0   **D**

% Daily Value*   **E**

F **Total Fat** 0g	**0%**
Saturated Fat 0g	**0%**
Trans Fat 0g	
G **Cholesterol** 0mg	**0%**
H **Sodium** 20mg	**1%**
Potassium 150mg	**4%**
I **Total Carbohydrate** 6g	**2%**
J Dietary Fiber 1g	**6%**
K Sugars 3g	
L **Protein** 2g	

M

Vitamin A 10%	•	Vitamin C 10%
Calcium 0%	•	Iron 4%

* Percent Daily Values are based on a 2,000 calorie diet.

N **INGREDIENTS:** ORGANIC TOMATOES.

O PROCESSED IN A FACILITY THAT ALSO PROCESSES MILK AND WHEAT.

A. **Serving Size:** A serving size is the amount of food that should be eaten in one serving. It is listed by a general household measurement, such as pieces, cups or ounces (i.e., 10 nuts or ½ cup of rice). Serving size is an important part of a healthy diet. Eating larger portions than the recommended amount will contribute to weight gain.

B. **Servings Per Container:** Sometimes that small package that you assume is one serving is really two or more. If manufacturers think that you will be scared off by the high number of calories, they sometimes make two servings out of what appears to be a single serving nutrition bar or bag of nuts. So, always check the number of servings as well as the calorie count.

C. **Calories:** The number of calories in a serving, not in the whole container.

D. **Calories From Fat:** The number of calories per serving that come from fat.

E. **Daily Value (% DV):** A healthy person should consume a certain amount of fats, carbohydrates, fiber, protein and vitamins and minerals each day. The nutrition label provides a list of percentages (called the Percent Daily Value) which tells you what percentage of your daily requirement of a given nutrient one serving of the food provides. The Percent Daily Value is based on a daily diet of 2,000 calories. Calorie adjustments must be made for age, gender and exercise level. See www.mypyramid.gov for more information.

F. **Total Fat:** The number of grams of fat per serving. The information is broken down into Saturated Fat and Trans Fat. Companies are allowed to list the amount of trans fat as 0 grams if one serving contains less than .5 grams of trans fat. Always check the ingredient list for trans fat, which may be listed as hydrogenated vegetable oil or partially hydrogenated vegetable oil.

G. **Cholesterol:** The number of grams of cholesterol per serving. You should pay close attention to this number if you have heart disease.

H. **Sodium:** Processed foods tend to be very high in sodium. Look closely to make sure your diet is not too high in it.

I. **Total Carbohydrate:** The number of grams of carbohydrates per serving.

J. **Dietary Fiber:** Fiber helps your body digest the food you eat, and it can help lower your risk of diabetes and heart disease. A food is considered high in fiber if it contains 5 grams of fiber or more per serving. Fiber is found in fruits, vegetables and whole grains.

K. **Sugars:** The total amount of sugar per serving. Sugars add calories, and are often listed on the label in other terms, such as "high fructose corn syrup," "dextrose," "invert sugar" or "turbinado." Pay extra attention to the ingredients list to be sure you are not consuming sugars that are not part of the LID.

L. **Protein:** The number of grams of protein per serving.

M. **Vitamins and Minerals:** The nutrition label lists vitamin A, vitamin C, calcium and iron. You should try to get more of these nutrients in your daily diet, as well as other vitamins and minerals that are not listed on the label.

N. **Ingredient List:** Manufacturers are required to list all of the ingredients contained in the product by weight and in order of amount, from most to least. A jar of tomato sauce with tomatoes as the first ingredient lets you know that tomatoes are the main ingredient. A spice or herb listed last is present in the least amount. This information is critical for anyone who has allergies, and for prudent shoppers who want more tomatoes than water, or whole foods rather than refined.

O. **Allergens:** Manufacturers will include a warning on the label if the food was made in a factory where foods containing allergens (such as nuts) have been processed on the same manufacturing lines.

Don't Be Confused By the Words Printed On the Labels

The foods we eat should be as close to their natural state as possible. You want to avoid products that have any fortified or enriched ingredients. For example, to ensure that the product you are buying is truly made entirely from whole grains, the label needs to specify "whole grain," rather than merely "with whole grain." "Made with whole wheat flour" doesn't mean the product is 100% whole grain.

Words such as "fresh," "no additives" and "natural" can also be confusing. They may look good, but these terms aren't regulated, so they don't necessarily mean a food is better for you.

How to Save

It is unfortunate that eating well and providing our bodies with the best possible nutrition comes at a much higher price tag than does eating convenient or processed foods. With savvy and a little extra effort, however, a whole foods diet need not be a financial burden. Below are 14 tips on how to save money when buying whole and/or organic foods.

1. **Make your own.** In the Sauces and Condiments and Pantry sections of this book (pages 232-273), you'll find some recipes that give you the option of making your own basic ingredients, which can save you a significant amount of money. For example, learn how to make your own almond and coconut milk. Additionally, lesser known grains, ground into flour, can be bought pre-packaged at any natural foods store, but the cost is often quite high. For the best possible bargain, you can buy the grain itself and grind your own flour for a fraction of the store price.

2. **Buy a coffee grinder.** Having a coffee grinder dedicated to items other than coffee beans will save you an extraordinary amount of money. Organic nut butters can cost more than $20 per jar! You can grind your own nut butters at home. After grinding your first few jars, the investment of an inexpensive coffee grinder will be more than paid for. In the pantry section (page 232), you'll find recipes that explain how to use a coffee grinder to make nut butters, flours and more.

3. **Pick your own.** A fun activity to share with friends and family is to go berry, apple or peach picking. There's nothing more delicious than freshly picked berries, and their lower-than-store price is an added bonus. Freeze blueberries or can peaches to use throughout the year.

4. **Grow your own.** If you have a green thumb, consider growing your own vegetable or herb garden. Plant your favorite herbs in pots so you can have them for cooking all year round. Grow an extra crop of your favorite vegetables, and can them to use throughout the winter.

5. **Join a CSA.** CSA, or community supported agriculture, gives consumers the opportunity to purchase a membership to cover production costs of local farmers. In exchange, consumers receive a weekly share of the farm's seasonal produce throughout the harvest period. Being a member of a CSA introduces new and different in-season vegetables to your diet, providing you with a wider range of nutrients.

6. **Shop at a farmers' market.** Farmers' markets are very popular and have similar advantages to a CSA: you can buy local, freshly picked produce, farm-fresh eggs, cheeses, meats, herbs and more. Prices are often less than you'd find at your local grocery store, and the food is usually fresher.

7. **Become a member.** A food co-op is a collectively owned grocery store that allows shoppers to become members. Some co-ops have special offers for members that are not available to the general public.

8. **Browse closeout stores.** Closeout stores are a great place to find affordable, delicious, organic foods. I buy my organic extra virgin olive oil at a local chain closeout store for $6.99 per bottle. Compare that price to the same-sized bottle at the grocery store, priced at a whopping $18.99. Make sure to check the expiration dates. See the Resources section (page 274) for more suggestions.

9. **Buy ingredients or foods online.** You'll be surprised at the variety of high quality, organic foods you can find online for a significant bargain. See the Resources section (page 274) for some sites to try out.

10. **Sign up for online savings.** Some stores have online programs that you can join by providing an email address. They offer perks like extra savings on certain days and printable coupons that are not published anywhere else.

11. **Take advantage of sales, circulars and coupons.** Stores run specials all the time, and when one of your favorite foods is on sale, buying in bulk is the way to go. If you have internet access, you can go online to sign up for coupons, or to look up the weekly specials. Just last month at my local natural foods store, organic almonds were discounted by $4.00 per pound. You never know what kind of deal you might snag by being an informed shopper.

12. **Know your prices.** Product prices can vary by dollars from one store to another. Develop a list of your favorite products and compile a price comparison for each store where you shop. You'll be surprised by how much you can save just by knowing what foods to buy at which store.

13. **Buy in bulk.** The savings from buying bulk over packaged can be substantial. Co-ops, natural food stores and some chain grocery stores offer foods in bulk. From nuts to grains to herbs, you can buy the amount that suits your needs.

14. **Ask for it.** A company wants nothing more than a new customer. If you would like to try a new product, but price is a factor, you can contact the company and tell them so. Often they will send you coupons or samples.

Part II

Getting Started

Before You Cook, Remember...

- Read the recipe thoroughly.

- Take time to learn the basic cooking techniques used in the recipe.

- Be sure you have all the ingredients assembled and enough time to prepare the recipe before you begin to cook. If you are missing ingredients, feel free to substitute something similar for the missing item.

- Always wash produce, grains and beans, even if they are organic. Vegetables that have an outer skin, such as melons and squash, should also be washed, because when you cut them, germs on the skin can spread into the edible portion.

- Always wash your hands before cooking, and after touching raw poultry.

- Wash cooking surfaces and place cutting boards in the dishwasher after preparing foods, especially poultry and meats. This will help ensure food safety.

- Always marinate food in the refrigerator, unless it marinates for less than 30 minutes, or the recipe specifically instructs otherwise.

Useful Kitchen Equipment

Baking

Cake pans: 8- or 9-inch round pans, used for cakes; or 8x8x2- or 9x9x2-inch square pans, used for brownies, bar cookies and general cooking and baking.

Cooling racks: Wire racks of assorted sizes, used to cool cakes, cookies and other baked goods.

Custard cups: Heat resistant cups (usually about 5 ounces in size) that can be placed in the oven, used to make individual servings of custard and pudding.

Flour sifters, with handles: Used to sift (remove lumps and lighten texture) flour (wire sieves can also be used for this purpose).

Loaf pans: 9x5x3- or 8½x4½x2½-inch pans, used for quick breads.

Muffin pans: 6- or 12-cup muffin pans, used for muffins.

Tart pans: 8-, 9- or 10-inch pans with removable bottoms, used for tarts and quiches.

Pie plates: 8-, 9- or 10-inch pans (also 9-inch deep dish pie plates), used for pies and quiches.

Springform pans: Pans of varying sizes (5- to 10-inch available) with removable bottoms and buckles that expand the pans' sides for easy cake removal, used for cheesecakes.

Mixers

Hand mixers: Used for light-duty mixing, although some of these mixers are very powerful and come with dough hooks.

Stand mixers: Heavy-duty mixers with detachable bowls, dough hooks and more powerful motors; can be used for long-term mixing and kneading.

Stick (immersion) blenders: Hand-held blenders that are used for blending soups, making smoothies and more.

Other kitchen equipment

Blenders and food processors: If you don't have both types of equipment, these two appliances can be used interchangeably. However, blenders are better for making homemade mayonnaise and for liquefying fruits and vegetables for drinks. Food processors are better for slicing, chopping and shredding large quantities of food in a few seconds.

Cheesecloth: Cheesecloth is light-weight cotton mesh cloth commonly used to strain foods. It can be purchased in the baking section of the grocery store, or by the yard at the fabric store.

Citrus zesters: used to remove the skins, commonly called the "zest," from citrus fruits).

Colanders: Used to drain water from pasta and cooked vegetables.

Cutting boards: Boards made from wood or plastic, used for cutting, chopping and many other kitchen tasks. For food safety reasons, you should have several cutting boards reserved for different purposes: one for meats, one for poultry and one for vegetables and fruits. Be sure to keep them clean and sanitized by washing them in the dishwasher, or with a mild solution of bleach.

Double boiler: Pot with a separate insert that fits into its top. To cook with a double boiler, fill the bottom section with 2 inches of water and bring the water almost to a boil. Place the food in the top of part of the double boiler, set it over the bottom section and cook as the recipe directs. If you don't have a double boiler, you can make one by using a bowl and a pot that fit together, so that the bowl rests in the pot without touching the pot's contents. Never allow the boiling or hot water in the bottom section of a double boiler to touch the bottom of the double boiler's top section.

Sieves/strainers: Usually made of fine, stainless steel mesh; can be used to drain liquid, or as sifters.

Measuring cups

Nesting measuring cups: A set of cups, which are known as "dry measure" cups because they are used to measure dry ingredients. A set usually consists of one each of ¼-cup, ⅓-cup, ½-cup and 1-cup measures. Some sets also include ¾-cup and ⅔-cup measures. You should own at least one set of measuring cups.

Graduated measuring cups: Glass or plastic cups with spouts and handles, in a variety of sizes from 1-cup to 10-cup, used to measure liquids. They are marked by ounces and by fractions of a cup: ¼-cup, ⅓ cup, ⅔-cup, ¾-cup and 1-cup.

Measuring spoons: A set of spoons, usually nesting and connected at the handles, used to measure small amounts from ¼-teaspoon up to 1-tablespoon.

Knives

Chef's knives: All-purpose knives with curved handles to allow the cook to rock the knife on the cutting board for a more precise cut.

Paring knives: Small, all-purpose knives with plain-edged blades, ideal for peeling and other small or intricate cutting.

Boning knives: Knives with thin, flexible blades, usually about 5- or 6-inches long, that can maneuver well in tight spaces, used to remove bones from cuts of meat.

Bread slicing knives: Serrated knives able to cut soft bread without crushing it.

Carving knives: Usually 12- to 15-inch blades, used to slice thin cuts of meat from poultry, roasts, hams and other large, cooked meats. Carving knives are much thinner than chef's knives, enabling them to carve thinner, more precise slices.

Slicing knives: Similar to carving knives, but generally longer and narrower, with either plain or serrated edges and either blunted or rounded tips.

Thermometers

Instant read thermometers: Inserted into meat at intervals during cooking, to measure the internal temperature and gauge the degree of doneness.

Fry thermometers: Marked with graduated temperatures and with temperatures indicated as ideal for frying, used for deep fat frying.

Oven thermometers: Placed on the oven rack to indicate the temperature in the oven at any given time; necessary because oven dial settings are not always accurate.

Cooking Methods

Below you will find definitions for various cooking methods and techniques used in recipes in this and other cookbooks.

Bake: Cook in an oven, usually in one that has been preheated.

Baste: Moisten roasting food, usually using the pan juices.

Beat: Combine a mixture until smooth by bringing the depths to the surface and vice-versa, usually using a mixer, wire whisk or spoon.

Blanch: Drop in boiling water for about a minute, usually done to remove the skin from fruits, vegetables or nuts.

Blend: Thoroughly combine two or more ingredients, usually using a spoon, wire whisk or electric mixer.

Boil: Heat a liquid until bubbles constantly rise to the surface (water boils at 212°F). A full, rolling boil is reached when stirring the liquid will not quell the bubbling. Most recipes instruct you to lower the heat once a liquid comes to a boil, at which lower temperature, the liquid will simmer.

Braise: Brown on all sides in a hot pan using a small amount of oil. After the food is browned, add liquid and cover the pan. Simmer until tender on medium to low heat. Braising is generally done to tenderize tougher cuts of meat.

Broil: Cook on the oven rack directly below the heating source, using a pan with a drip tray. In outdoor broiling, cook directly above the heated coals.

Caramelize: Use intense dry heat, as in roasting or sautéing, to break down the natural sugars contained in all meats and vegetables, resulting in brown color and rich flavor.

Chop: Cut into roughly equal-sized pieces — either coarse larger-sized pieces, or finely chopped, smaller-sized pieces.

Coat: Evenly cover with a substance, such as flour, breadcrumbs or sugar.

Cool: Allow to stand at room temperature until no longer warm.

Cream: Combine softened shortening, butter or margarine with sugar until the mixture is light and fluffy, usually using an electric mixer.

Cube: Cut into equal-sized pieces, such as ½-inch pieces.

Cut in: Use two knives or a pastry cutter to slice fat, such as butter, into flour until the fat and flour form pea-sized pieces.

Dice: Cut into very small (¼-inch) cubes.

Dissolve: Mix a dry substance into a liquid until it forms a solution.

Dot: Scatter small pieces (usually of butter or margarine) over the surface.

Dredge: Coat lightly with a substance, such as flour, sugar or breadcrumbs.

Fold: Incorporate into a mixture by using an under-over motion, often using a rubber spatula. Most often, recipes will instruct you to fold beaten egg whites into a mixture. Unlike stirring, which breaks up the egg whites and causes them to deflate, folding egg whites incorporates air into the mixture.

Grate: Shred into small uniform pieces, using a grater, zester or the grating disc of a food processor.

Grease: Rub the surface of a pan with butter, margarine or shortening, or spray with non-stick cooking spray. Greasing helps keep food from sticking to the pan, and makes removing food from the pan easier.

Marinate: Let stand in a marinade mixture for a prescribed period of time, usually in order to flavor and/or tenderize meat.

Mince: Cut very fine.

Pan-broil: Cook uncovered in an ungreased or lightly greased frying pan, pouring off any accumulated fat.

Pan-fry: Cook in a frying pan using a small amount of hot fat.

Par-boil: Cook or boil partially. Parboiling is usually a preliminary part of the cooking process, with parboiled foods later being fried, baked or roasted.

Pare: Remove the skin or outer coating of a fruit or vegetable.

Peel: Remove the skin or outer coating of a fruit, such as a banana or orange, usually by hand.

Preheat: Heat an oven or griddle to a desired temperature before using it for baking or cooking.

Pulse: Process or blend in a food processor or blender by holding down the "on" button for a second or two, and then releasing.

Purée: Reduce to paste or a sauce-like consistency, using a blender, food processor or food mill.

Sauté: Cook in a small amount of hot fat.

Score: Cut shallow slits in the surface.

Sear: Brown the surface quickly over high heat in a frying pan, or on a griddle or grill pan.

Season: Sprinkle with salt, pepper, herbs and/or spices.

Shallow fry: Cook in an inch or two of hot fat.

Sift: Pass through a flour sifter or sieve, in order to make a substance (usually flour) lighter and to remove any lumps.

Simmer: Cook just below the boiling point, at about 185°F.

Sliver: Cut into long, thin pieces.

Snip: Cut with kitchen shears/scissors.

Stir: Blend with a spoon in a circular motion, widening the circle until all the ingredients are incorporated.

Thicken: Blend a thickening agent, such as arrowroot, cornstarch or flour, with a small amount of liquid until it forms a smooth paste. Whisk the resulting paste into the liquid to be thickened and continue to stir (usually while heating to a boil) until the liquid becomes thick.

Toss: Mix lightly with two forks, or a fork and spoon, usually done to coat salad greens with dressing.

Whip: Beat with an electric mixer or wire whisk, in order to incorporate air and increase volume.

Zest: Zest is the thin outer skin of a citrus fruit and contains the essential oils of the fruit. It adds the flavor of the fruit, without the acid.

LID Food Glossary

Some of the ingredients used in this book are not generally a part of most peoples' diets. Below, we have defined some of the lesser-known foods and have noted the nutritional value of some of the foods that are exceptionally good for you.

Grains

Buckwheat is a fruit in the rhubarb family. It is not a grain, and does not contain wheat or gluten. It is very high in protein and a good source of manganese, magnesium and dietary fiber.

Durum is hard, dense, high protein wheat that's high in gluten, which makes it an ideal wheat for premium pasta products.

Einkorn means "one grain" in German. It's an ancient, one-seeded wheat (Triticum monococcum) that's grown in arid regions and is native to Southwest Asia.

Farro is a type of wheat that's more easily digestible than most wheat. Farro has been cultivated in the Mediterranean and Middle East for thousands of years, where it's still very popular. It is rich in minerals and vitamins, antioxidants, phytonutrients, lignans and betaine. Betaine, when combined with choline, has been shown to prevent or reduce stress-induced inflammation.

Groats are grains, such as oats, wheat, barley or buckwheat, with their hulls only partially removed, leaving a coarse grain that's higher in nutritional value and natural fiber than more refined cereals. Because groats are less refined, they take longer to prepare than do other breakfast cereals.

Kamut is a grain that's closely related to wheat, but is similar to spelt, in that it contains lower levels of gluten than wheat, and so might be better tolerated by individuals with wheat and gluten sensitivities.

Millet is an ancient, wheat- and gluten-free grain that retains its alkaline properties after being cooked. It's rich in B vitamins, iron and other important minerals, and is also considered to be a good source of protein.

Quinoa is often thought to be a grain; however, it is not a grain, but is rather the gluten-free seed of a leafy plant that's distantly related to spinach. Quinoa has excellent reserves of protein and, unlike most grains, is not missing the amino acid lysine, which provides you with a more complete protein.

Recipes for Repair: A Lyme Disease Cookbook

Semolina is a coarsely ground flour, usually made from hard durum wheat or maize. Semolina is what's left behind when the finer flour has been sifted out. It's used in making pasta, breakfast cereals and puddings.

Spelt is an ancient grain in the wheat family and contains less gluten than wheat. Some individuals with gluten sensitivity can often tolerate this grain.

Teff is an ancient, gluten-free, African whole grain cereal. It is the smallest of all grains. There are two types of teff, ivory and dark. Ivory teff is higher in protein, while dark teff has higher levels of iron. Both varieties are high in calcium and zinc, with the nutrition concentrated in the germ and the bran. When cooked, teff makes a nutritious breakfast cereal with the consistency and texture of wheat farina. When milled into flour, teff can be used in baking.

Fats

Expeller Pressed Oil is oil extracted by pressing the seed without the use of chemical solvents.

Ghee is clarified butter. In the clarifying process the butter is heated and milk solids are removed, leaving the butter oil without the lactose and casein that people with dairy sensitivity cannot tolerate. See page 234 for instructions on how to make your own ghee.

Palm Oil is a tropical oil. Long perceived as unhealthy, palm oil is actually a beneficial fat source when used in its natural form. Palm oil is indeed high in saturated fatty acids, but these are actually good for you. Unrefined palm oil remains a much healthier oil than any hydrogenated vegetable oil. Palm kernel oil, however, is heavily processed and entirely different than palm oil and in general is unhealthy and should be avoided.

Safflower Oil is oil expeller pressed from the seeds of the safflower plant, which is a member of the sunflower family. Safflower oil is often used for cooking, because it is healthier than most other oils.

Sweeteners

Agave Nectar is an extract from the agave plant. It is low on the glycemic index, has a sweet, consistent flavor and dissolves quickly in cool or hot foods.

Lakanto is an all-natural, zero calorie sweetener with a glycemic index value of zero. It's made from a proprietary blend of the sweet extract of the Chinese-grown fruit, luo han guo. See the Resources section (page 274) for more information.

Raw Honey is a natural antimicrobial and antioxidant. It enhances the immune and digestive systems because of the various amino acids, minerals and beneficial live enzymes found naturally in raw honey. "Raw" means it has never been pasteurized, filtered or heated, all of which destroy these powerful nutrients. In the many recipes in this book that call for raw honey, it is never heated above 117°F, so as not to damage the enzymes. If you plan to cook with honey at temperatures above 117° F, use regular honey, rather than raw.

Sorbitol is a low-calorie sweetener known as a sugar alcohol, or polyol. It is non-carcinogenic, and is about 60% as sweet as sucrose, with one-third fewer calories. It may be useful to people with diabetes. Sorbitol is found naturally in prunes and apricots. It is also commercially made for use in chewing gum and sugar-free sweets, and may also be used in baking and cooking. It has a smooth mouth feel and a sweet, cool, pleasant taste. Sorbitol should not be used in excess, because it can act as a laxative and may produce flatulence and gastric upset.

Stevia is a bush (Stevia rebaudiana Bertoni), the leaves of which are used to produce extracts with up to 300 times the sweetness of sugar. The powdered version of this sweetener has a different level of sweetness than the extract, so check the stevia product you are using to see what its sweetening power is, and what recipes are recommended for it. A conversion chart available from the manufacturer can help you convert the amount of sugar in your recipes to the appropriate amount of stevia. You can bake with stevia because it is stable to 392°F, but because its sweetness is so concentrated, substituting the correct amount is crucial. None of the recipes in this book use stevia because of potential confusion from the wide variety of stevia products available. If you want to substitute stevia for a given sweetener in these recipes, check the equivalent amount of sugar for the given sweetener, and then substitute the amount of stevia appropriate for that quantity of sugar.

Xylitol, like sorbitol, is a sugar alcohol. It differs from other sweeteners, such as sorbitol, fructose and glucose, in that its molecule has five, rather than six carbon atoms. Xylitol's sweetening power is the same as that of sucrose (table sugar), which is why it was chosen as the sweetener for some of the recipes in this book. If you prefer not to use xylitol, it will be easy for you to determine the appropriate amount of alternate sweetener because xylitol is the same as sugar in sweetness. Simply check your desired sweetener's conversion rate with sugar, and use that amount of the substitute sweetener in the recipe. Like sorbitol, xylitol can act as a laxative and may produce flatulence and gastric upset if used in excess. Until you know how this sweetener affects you, limit its use to one recipe a day at most (in fact, this is a good precaution to take with all sweeteners ending in -tol).

Thickeners

Arrowroot is a neutral-flavored spice used in cooking as a thickening agent. It can be found in co-ops, health food stores or online (see resource section).

Tapioca (Cassava) is a starch extracted from the root of the cassava or yucca plant. It is granular and is frequently used to thicken puddings.

Guar Gum is the ground-up extract of the guar bean, which comes from a plant grown primarily in India. **Xanthan Gum** is a corn-based fermented product. Both of these gluten-free gums help hold gluten-free baked goods together, which would otherwise crumble. Guar gum is the less expensive of the two, and is the best option if you are sensitive to corn, but these gums can be used interchangeably. Recipes typically call for very small amounts of these products, which can be found in the bulk section of your local co-op or health food store, and thus can be purchased in small quantities.

Sea Vegetables

Arame, Dulse, Hijiki, Kelp, Kombu, Nori and Wakame are the most common edible seaweeds and have a salty (and sometimes spicy) taste that adds flavor and nutrition to soups, stews and salads. They are nature's richest sources of iodine and contain high levels of vitamin K, folate, magnesium and other trace minerals. Lignans, which are plant compounds that may help ward off some serious health threats such as cancer, are found in these super foods of the sea. Vegans especially should turn to sea vegetables, as they are an excellent source of vitamin B12, a nutrient mostly found in meat. Refer to the package for cooking and rehydration instruction.

Traditional Soy Products

Miso and **Natto** are traditional fermented soy products. Miso is a thick, paste-like substance, whereas natto retains the soybean-shape and has a stringier texture. Both provide you with high levels of protein and a low calorie count.

Tamari is the liquid that's collected from miso as it ages. Tamari is used like soy sauce.

Tempeh is made by a natural culturing and controlled fermentation process that binds soybeans into a cake form. Originating in Indonesia, tempeh is high in protein and very easy to digest.

Other

Raw Apple Cider Vinegar differs from apple cider vinegar in that it has never been filtered, heated or pasteurized. These processes destroy the "Mother of Vinegar," which is the organic matter that results from the fermentation process. Raw apple cider vinegar aids in detoxification and is rich in natural minerals, vitamins and enzymes.

Kefir is similar to yogurt, but contains more strains of beneficial bacteria. These healthy bacteria can actually colonize in the intestinal tract, while those from yogurt do not. Kefir is traditionally made from cow or goat's milk. When buying kefir, be sure you are buying the unsweetened variety.

Coconut Kefir is fermented coconut water from young coconuts. This water contains minerals, vitamins, antioxidants, amino acids and enzymes. It also has a high sugar content, and when the water is fermented, the sugars are converted into probiotics, which are an especially important addition to your diet when you are taking antibiotics. You can buy ready-made coconut kefir, or you can make your own using a culture starter kit. See the Resources section (page 274)to learn about the options.

Sprouted Grain Breads are flourless breads made from grains and legumes (most often including wheat, millet and spelt) that are sprouted before being ground into flour. Sprouted grains have increased vitamins and nutrients and are almost always organic. Some varieties of sprouted grain bread also use sprouted lentils and sprouted soybeans, making the bread a complete protein. For example, Ezekiel bread incorporates legumes and also uses a special baking process to preserve even more valuable nutrients. Although not always sold under refrigeration, sprouted grain breads should be refrigerated or frozen until use. Because they are made without preservatives, they have a shorter shelf life.

Herbes de Provence is a mixture of herbs invented in the 1970s. It generally includes a combination of thyme, oregano, marjoram, bay leaf, basil and rosemary. The Mediterranean flavor of these herbs goes well with meat, poultry, game, vegetables and tomato-based and grilled dishes. Many of the recipes in this book call for this blend. If you do not have this blend, you can make it yourself using a small amount of any or all of these seasonings.

Nuts and Seeds

High in fiber and protein, nuts and seeds are not only delicious, but are extremely nutritious. Nuts and some seeds contain an enzyme-inhibiting substance which make them difficult to digest. Soaking removes this layer and stimulates the process of germination, which increases the nutrients. An alternative to soaking is to dry roast. This also increases the vitamin content, although not as much as germination.

Buying

Buy raw nuts and seeds in bulk for the most affordable prices.

Germination

Soaking: Combine sea salt with filtered water in a large bowl. The salt activates enzymes that neutralize the enzyme inhibitors. Add the nuts to the water (the water level should be two to three inches over the top of the nuts). Soak at room temperature for the time specified in the chart below. Drain well before drying.

Drying: Drying time can vary, depending on the nut or seed. Lay nuts out on a baking sheet and bake them at 150°F, or dry them in a dehydrator until they are dry and crispy. Refer to the chart below for general drying guidelines.

Nut or seed	Soak time (at room temperature)	Sea salt	Drying time [2]
Almonds	8 to 12 hours	1 tablespoon	12 to 24 hours
Cashews (whole)	4 hours (no longer than 6 hours)	1 tablespoon	6 to 12 hours
Peanuts, pecans, walnuts	7 hours to overnight	2 teaspoons	12 to 24 hours
Pumpkin seeds	7 hours to overnight	2 tablespoons	12 to 24 hours
All others	6 to 24 hours	Varies	12 to 24 hours

Toasting

Spread nuts on a baking pan and cook in a preheated 350°F oven for a few minutes. Not all nuts cook in the same amount of time, so watch them closely as they can burn very quickly.

Storage

Nuts have a high fat content so they can become rancid. They should be stored in air-tight containers away from heat, light or humidity. If you buy in bulk, keep a small amount on hand for cooking or snacking. Store the remainder in air-tight containers in either the refrigerator or freezer. Nuts freeze very well and defrost in just minutes.

[1] Not all ovens can be set at temperatures as low as 150°F. Drying at higher temperatures will destroy the good enzymes created by the germination process.

[2] Drying times vary. Be sure nuts are fully dry to avoid the possibility of mold growing.

Beans, Peas and Lentils

Dried beans, peas and lentils are an excellent source of protein, dietary fiber and complex carbohydrates. Also called legumes or pulses, they are flavorful, nutritionally dense, inexpensive and versatile, and are a great alternative protein source for vegetarians. Cooking dried beans takes more time than opening a can, but dried beans are more flavorful, have a more pleasing texture and are cheaper than canned beans.

Always Do the Following Before Cooking Dried Beans

Sort: Arrange dried beans on a sheet pan or clean kitchen towel, and sort through them to pick out any shriveled or broken beans, stones or debris.

Rinse: Thoroughly rinse the sorted beans in cold, running water.

Soak: Soaking beans before cooking is vital for digestibility. The quick soak method, described below, is the preferable soaking method, as it is more effective in reducing the hard-to-digest sugars that cause gastrointestinal upset. Never cook beans in the same water used to soak them.

Two Methods for Soaking

Quick soak: Put the beans in a large pot and cover them with two to three inches of cool, clean water. Bring to a boil, and then boil briskly for two to three minutes. Remove from the heat, cover the pot and let sit for one hour. Rinse and drain well before cooking.

Regular soak: Put the beans in a large bowl and cover them with two to three inches of cool, filtered water. Let sit at room temperature for eight hours or overnight, and then rinse and drain well before cooking.

Suggested Cooking Methods

Stovetop: Put the beans in a large pot and cover them with two inches of water or stock. Don't add salt at this point, since that will slow the beans' softening. Slowly bring to a boil, skimming off any foam that collects on the surface. Reduce the heat, cover the pot and simmer, stirring occasionally and adding more liquid if necessary, until the beans are tender when mashed or pierced with a fork. Cooking time is generally about one to two hours, but may vary depending on the variety, age and size of the beans used.

Slow cooking: Put the soaked beans in the slow cooker with the other recipe ingredients, and add a two-inch strip of kombu, rather than salt. The kombu will help make the beans more digestible.

Storage

Uncooked: Keep dried beans, peas and lentils in airtight containers and store them in a dry, cool, dark place. Beans stored this way will keep for up to a year, and peas and lentils will keep for up to six months.

Cooked: Refrigerate cooked beans in a covered container for up to 5 days. Beans freeze very well and will last for up to 6 months in an airtight freezer container.

Peas and Lentils

Sort and rinse dried peas and lentils as you would dried beans. Bring one-and-a-half cups of water per cup of peas or lentils to a boil. Once the water boils, add the peas or lentils, return to a boil and then reduce the heat and simmer, partially covered, until tender (30-45 minutes).

When making soups and stews, you do not need to precook peas or lentils. Simply add them uncooked, but be sure to add enough liquid because they will absorb liquid as they cook.

Preparation of Beans, Peas and Lentils

Refer to the chart below for guidelines on cooking time, water amount and yield for one cup of dried beans, peas or lentils, as well as information on whether or not they need to be soaked.

Bean, pea or lentil	Presoak	Water (cups)	Stovetop cook time	Approximate yield (cups)
Black beans	yes	3 cups	60 to 90 minutes	2¼ cups
Black-eyed peas	no	3 cups	45 to 60 minutes	2 cups
Cannellini beans	yes	3-4 cups	60 to 90 minutes	2½ cups
Garbanzo beans	yes	4 cups	90 to 150 minutes	2 cups
Great Northern beans	yes	3-4 cups	60 to 90 minutes	2½ cups
Kidney beans	yes	3 cups	60 to 90 minutes	2 cups
Lentils, green or brown	no	1 ½ cups	30 to 40 minutes	2¼ cups
Lentils, red	no	3 cups	15 to 30 minutes	2 cups
Lentils, French or black	no	1 ½ cups	20 to 30 minutes	2 cups
Navy beans	yes	3-4 cups	90 to 120 minutes	2 cups
Split peas (green)	no	3-4 cups	50 to 60 minutes	2 cups
Split peas (yellow)	no	3-4 cups	50 to 60 minutes	2 cups
Pinto beans	yes	3 cups	90 to 120 minutes	2¾ cups
Soybeans	yes	4 cups	3 to 4 hours	2 cups

Whole Grains

Whole grains and whole grain flours have more flavor than refined white flour, because when grains are milled to make refined flours, up to 80% of the grain's nutrients are removed, along with most of its characteristic nutty flavor and chewy texture. See page 242 to learn how to make your own flours.

When you eat a whole grain, you ingest the complete form of the grain, which means that you get all of its vitamins and nutrients and enjoy its complex texture and rich taste. Whole grains include: the bran, which is an important source of most of the B-complex vitamins and of fiber, and which adds body, texture and flavor to the grain; the germ, which contains minerals, B vitamins, protein, vitamin E and oils; and finally, the endosperm, which consists mostly of starch, as well as some protein and other nutrients.

Buying: Look for grains with undamaged kernels, because the outer bran layer protects the kernel's flavor and nutrients from destruction by light and air.

Storing: Store whole grains in airtight containers in a cool, dry place out of direct light.

Using: Use whole grains such as oatmeal and 7-grain cereal for breakfast. Use whole grains such as millet and quinoa as dinner side dishes and in salads.

Always check the cooking and storing instructions on the packaging before preparing whole grains. The following are general instructions:

Rinse: Immediately prior to cooking, thoroughly rinse whole grains in cold water until water runs clear, and then strain them to remove any dirt or debris.

Cook: As a general rule, you can cook whole grains by simply boiling water (or broth, for added flavor), adding the grain and returning to a boil, and then lowering the heat and simmering, covered, until tender.

Gluten Level in Certain Grains		
None	*Low*	*High*
Amaranth, Brown Rice, Buckwheat, Corn, Millet, Quinoa, Sorghum, Teff, Wild Rice	Barley, Faro, Kamut, Oats*, Rye, Spelt	Durum, Wheat, Einkorn, Semolina
* If you are gluten intolerant, be sure the package says gluten-free.		

Test: Just like pasta, always test for doneness a minute before the estimated cooking time. Most whole grains should be slightly chewy when cooked.

Fluff: When grains are done cooking, remove them from the heat and gently fluff them with a fork. Then, cover them and set them aside to sit for five to ten minutes before serving.

Gluten is the substance in some grains that gives dough (made from particular grains) its elasticity and helps bread to rise properly. Many people have gluten intolerances, but in varying degrees. Some can tolerate low levels of gluten.

Fats

Grades of Olive Oil

Extra virgin olive oil comes from the first cold pressing of the olives, done by methods that do not refine the oil. The word "cold" is important because if heat is used, the olive oil's chemistry is changed. It also means that no chemicals have been used in the extraction of the oil. Extra virgin olive oil is judged to have a superior taste because its acidity rate of less than 1%.

Like extra virgin olive oil, there is no refined oil in virgin olive oil. Virgin olive oil has an acidity rate of less than 2%, and is judged to have a good taste.

Oils labeled as pure olive oil, olive oil, 100% pure olive oil and light olive oil are all refined oils. Bear in mind, all olive oil contains 120 calories per tablespoon. The only olive oils used in the LID are extra virgin olive oil and virgin olive oil.

Smoke Point

Some oils are better for high temperature cooking than others, because it is important that an oil not reach its smoke point during cooking. The smoke point generally refers to the temperature at which a cooking fat or oil begins to break down into glycerol and free fatty acids. The smoke point also marks the beginning of both flavor and nutritional degradation.

The higher an oil's smoke point, the better it is for high temperature cooking. Oils with similar smoke points are interchangeable in the recipes. The only stipulation is that any fat or oil you wish to substitute for a given oil must be permitted in whichever Phase you are in. Check the list of allowable foods at the beginning of each Phase.

Refer to the product's label for exact recommendations on ideal cooking temperatures, as they differ from product to product.

Lentil Soup, page 122

Part III

Recipes for Repair:
A Lyme Disease Cookbook

Poached Eggs Florentine with Béarnaise Sauce, page 74

Phase 1
Contents

Phase 1: The Induction Phase *(one week)*

Phase 1 of the Lyme Inflammation Diet® is to be followed for one week. Its goal is to help your body quickly shut down the mechanisms of chronic inflammation and begin detoxifying, which is accomplished by a primarily vegetarian diet consisting of safe foods low in what we call "universal negative inflammation triggers" (UNITs). Examples of UNITs include trans-fatty acids, AGEs and refined sugar. Exclusively consuming these Phase 1 fiber-rich foods will help your body to quickly and effectively begin to control inflammation. During this (and every) Phase, you should also avoid eating all foods to which you know you are allergic or sensitive, even if they are on this list.

In addition to restricting yourself to the foods permitted in Phase 1, you should strive to consume more servings of some of the allowable foods than others. Try to eat at least 5-8 servings of vegetables and 2-3 servings of fruit each day. Almonds, walnuts, pine nuts and freshly ground flaxseed are all good choices, as they are rich in anti-inflammatory oils and other nutrients.

During Phase 1, it's best to drink pure, filtered water, but you may also have unsweetened fruit juices from the allowable beverages list. Either juice them yourself, or buy high-quality fruit juices that contain no added sugar or artificial ingredients.

Other than eggs, fish is your primary source of protein during Phase 1. Except for sardines (usually sold canned), select fish that are wild-caught rather than farm-raised, as farm-raised fish are often full of antibiotics and coloring dyes. Do not fry fish (or eggs), as fried foods significantly contribute to inflammation in the body.

Modifying Fruit Consumption While Using Antibiotics

When taking antibiotics, you should generally limit your intake of most fruits because their naturally high sugar content can lead to yeast overgrowth in the intestinal system.

An unfortunate side effect of antibiotics is the death of healthy bacteria along with the unhealthy. Healthy bacteria help prevent the uncontrolled growth of potentially harmful organisms such as yeast, so their absence sets the stage for intestinal yeast infection. Because yeast feeds on sugar – even that from healthy fruits – the combination of antibiotics and fruit can lead to serious problems.

Therefore, when following the LID while taking antibiotics, observe these additional guidelines:

Eat Phase 1 fruits only two to three times per week.
Eat Phase 2 fruits only one to two times per week.
In Phase 3, eat low-sugar fruits, such as lemon, lime and grapefruit, daily if desired.

Any time you're taking antibiotics, also take probiotics to replace the friendly bacteria. *(See the sidebar on page 38 for more on probiotics.)*

Foods Allowed During Phase 1

Beverages [1]
Acai juice
Blackberry juice
Blueberry juice
Cherry juice [2]
Cranberry juice
Pomegranate juice [2]
Pure water
Raspberry juice

Fruits
Avocado
Blackberries
Blueberries
Cherries [2]
Coconut (or
  coconut milk)[3]
Cranberries
Green apple NEW
Pomegranate [2]
Raspberry

Nuts and Seeds
Almonds (or
  almond milk) [3]
Flaxseed
Pine nuts
Walnuts

Vegetables
Artichoke
Arugula
Asparagus
Beets
Bok choy
Broccoli
Cauliflower
Brussels sprouts

Cabbage
Carrots
Celery
Chard
Collard greens
Cucumber
Kale
Leeks
Mushrooms (shiitake
  are the best choice)
Mustard greens
Onions
Lettuce
Scallions
Spinach
Sprouts
String beans
Watercress

Grains
Brown rice
Wild rice

Protein
Eggs (organic, free-
  range recommended)
Flounder
Mackerel
Salmon
Sardines
Sole
Tilapia

Herbs and Spices
Baking soda NEW
Basil
Bay leaf NEW
Cardamom

Chives
Cilantro
Cinnamon
Cloves
Cream of tartar NEW
Cumin NEW
Curry
Garlic
Ginger
Lemon grass NEW
Mint NEW
Mustard [4] NEW
Mustard powder NEW
Mustard seed NEW
Oregano
Parsley
Rosemary
Sage NEW
Sea salt
Thyme NEW

Fats
Coconut oil NEW
Extra virgin olive oil [5]
Ghee
Virgin olive oil NEW

Sweeteners
Lakanto NEW
Raw honey [2,6]
Stevia

Other
Almond extract NEW
Apple cider vinegar
Coconut extract NEW
Mint extract NEW
Vanilla extract

---

[1] Unsweetened fruit juice only.

[2] Use sparingly, as they are very high in sugar.

[3] Read label closely as sweeteners and/or stabilizers are often added. It's best to make your own. See page 237 for recipe.

[4] Mustard is not permitted until Phase 3 because most mustards are made with varieties of vinegar other than apple cider. Some varieties of mustard are made with apple cider vinegar, however, making them allowable for Phase 1. (See the Resources section on page 274). Additionally, dry mustard can be substituted for prepared mustard at a ratio of one teaspoon dry for every one tablespoon prepared.

[5] Mixed with a small amount of sesame oil is also acceptable.

[6] Limit to two teaspoons per day. If you are unsure about the difference between honey and raw honey, see page 57.

Sautéed Asparagus Omelet

This omelet uses asparagus, but if you don't like asparagus or it isn't in season, you may substitute steamed broccoli.

Prep time: 15 minutes
Cook time: 10 minutes

Makes: 2 servings

1-2 tablespoons extra virgin olive oil

6 asparagus spears (5 ounces), cut into 1-inch pieces (discard tough ends)

½ small onion, chopped

1 clove garlic, crushed

3 eggs, beaten

1 teaspoon freshly chopped herbs

¼ teaspoon sea salt

1. Heat 1 tablespoon of the oil in a medium-sized frying pan over medium-high heat for 1 minute, or until hot.

2. Add the asparagus and sauté for 3 minutes, or until just tender.

3. Add the onion and sauté for 2 minutes, or until it begins to brown.

4. Add the garlic and sauté for 1 minute.

5. Add the remaining oil, if needed.

6. Pour the beaten eggs over the vegetables.

7. Combine the herbs and salt and sprinkle over the mixture. Allow it to set for about 30 seconds.

8. Lift the edges of the omelet and tilt the skillet, allowing any uncooked egg mixture to flow underneath. Continue to cook for about 2 minutes, or until the eggs are set.

9. Fold the omelet over and remove from the skillet. Serve immediately.

Cook's Note: This recipe can be doubled to make enough for dinner for the whole family. Serve with salad for a full meal. These omelets also reheat well, so save your leftovers for lunch.

Poached Eggs Florentine with Béarnaise Sauce

This recipe is perfect if you are hosting brunch, or if you just want to relax and enjoy a day at home.

Prep time: 30 minutes
(including sauce preparation)

Cook time: 15-20 minutes

Makes: 4 servings

1 recipe Béarnaise Sauce
(page 253)

1 tablespoon Ghee (page
234) or extra virgin olive
oil

1 small shallot, minced

1 small clove garlic,
crushed

1 bag (1 pound) baby
spinach

3 cups water

4 eggs

1 teaspoon raw apple cider
vinegar

Chopped parsley (optional)

1. Prepare the Béarnaise Sauce and set aside.

2. Heat the ghee or oil in a small frying pan.

3. Add the shallot and garlic and sauté over medium heat for 2 minutes, or until limp.

4. Add the spinach and sauté for 2 minutes, or until just limp. Set aside.

5. Pour the water into a frying pan, and bring it to a boil.

6. Crack each egg into a separate custard cup.

7. Once the water boils, add the vinegar and stir vigorously until a whirlpool forms.

8. Add the eggs one at a time, and poach for about 2 minutes.* Spoon any floating egg white back over the poaching egg. Continue until all the eggs are poached.

9. If necessary, reheat the spinach for a minute. Divide the spinach and place on four plates. Top each portion of spinach with a poached egg, and spoon Béarnaise Sauce over each. Garnish with chopped parsley if desired.

* Cooking time for the eggs is a matter of personal preference. The cooking time given here will result in runny yolks. Cook longer if you prefer firmer yolks.

Cook's Note: If you are making the Béarnaise Sauce in advance, you can reheat it over a double boiler, or on low in your microwave. When using a double boiler, be very careful never to let the water boil, or to let the hot water touch the bottom of the top section, as this will cause the sauce to curdle.

Carrot Almond Pancakes

These pancakes may look a little different than what you're used to, but they taste sweet, nutty and very satisfying. Top them with a teaspoon of raw honey and some blueberries for a complete breakfast treat.

Prep time: 10 minutes

Cook time: 12 minutes

. . . .

Makes: 4 pancakes

. . . .

1 cup peeled and grated carrots (2-3 carrots)

¼ cup almonds

1 slice fresh ginger (⅛-inch thick)

1 teaspoon ground flaxseed

2 tablespoons unsweetened shredded coconut

½ teaspoon ground cinnamon

1 egg

¼ teaspoon sea salt

½ teaspoon vanilla

1-2 tablespoons Ghee (page 234)

1 teaspoon raw honey

Blueberries (optional)

1. Place the grated carrots in a medium-sized bowl.
2. Place the almonds, ginger and flaxseed in the bowl of a food processor. Pulse 5-6 times until the almonds are finely ground.
3. Add the almond mixture and all of the remaining ingredients, except for the ghee, honey and blueberries, to the grated carrots.
4. Heat the ghee in a small frying pan over medium heat for 2 minutes, or until hot.
5. Pour two ¼-cup portions of pancake batter into the frying pan, and cook for about 3 minutes per side, or until lightly browned. Repeat with the remaining batter.
6. Top with honey and blueberries if desired, and serve hot.

Cook's Note: Prepare and refrigerate the pancake batter the night before, so that you can make your breakfast in a few minutes.

Coconut Berry Smoothie

This recipe makes enough for two smoothies, so share with someone, or take the extra to work for a mid-afternoon snack.

Prep time: 5 minutes

Makes: 2 drinks (3 cups)

1 cup **Coconut Milk (page 237)**

½ cup **unsweetened pomegranate or unsweetened pomegranate blueberry juice**

½ cup **blueberries**

½ cup **raspberries or blackberries**

2 teaspoons **raw honey**

½ cup **ice**

1. Place all the ingredients in a blender container in the order listed. Blend on High, or on a frozen drink setting, until the ice is crushed and the fruits are blended.

Cherry Vanilla Almond Blast

Cherries have a short season, but that doesn't mean that you can't enjoy this smoothie year-round. Frozen cherries are a fine substitute for fresh.

Prep time: 5 minutes

Makes: 1 drink

1 cup **frozen or fresh pitted cherries**

1 teaspoon **ground flaxseed**

¾ cup **Almond Milk (page 237)**

½ teaspoon **vanilla**

⅛ teaspoon **almond extract**

1 teaspoon **raw honey**

½ cup **ice cubes**

1. Place all the ingredients in a blender container. Cover, and blend until smooth.
2. Pour into a tall glass and serve immediately.

Cook's Note: If you don't like cherries, substitute raspberries, blueberries or any other fruit that is permitted in Phase 1.

Steamed Vegetables and Brown and Wild Rice with Fresh Herb Vinaigrette

Leftover rice and vegetables make a great salad when topped with Fresh Herb Vinaigrette.

Prep time: 15 minutes

Makes: 4 servings

2 cups cooked brown and wild rice

3 ounces steamed green beans

1 cup steamed bok choy

1 cup steamed julienned carrots

Fresh Herb Vinaigrette
¼ cup apple cider vinegar

1 teaspoon each freshly chopped basil and parsley

½ teaspoon freshly chopped tarragon or thyme

½ teaspoon dry mustard

¼ teaspoon each garlic powder and onion powder

1 teaspoon raw honey

¼ teaspoon sea salt

⅓ cup extra virgin olive oil

1. Place the cooked rice on a serving plate and top with the green beans, bok choy and carrots.
2. Combine all of the ingredients for the vinaigrette.
3. Spoon a small amount of the vinaigrette over the vegetables, and serve the remaining vinaigrette on the side.

Cook's Note: Any cooked vegetables can be used in this recipe. Use whatever you have on hand, or your family's favorites. It's a perfect way to use up your leftovers.

Pickled Beets

Pickled beets are great as an addition to a salad, or as a stand-alone side dish served hot or cold.

Prep time: 10 minutes

Cook time: 1 hour

Makes: 4-6 servings

1 bunch (4-5) beets (about 2 pounds worth)

¼ cup cider vinegar

½ cup water

1 small onion, sliced

1 clove garlic, peeled and thinly sliced

½ teaspoon sea salt

2 tablespoons raw honey

1. Place the beets in a quart saucepan and cover them with water. Cover the pan, and bring to a boil over high heat. Lower the heat to medium-high and cook for 45-50 minutes, or until a knife inserted in the middle of a beet comes out easily.

2. Drain, cool and peel the beets, and then slice them into ¼-inch thick slices.

3. Return the sliced beets to the saucepan and add the vinegar, water, onion, garlic and salt.

4. Cook over high heat until the mixture comes to a boil. Lower the heat and cook for about 10 minutes, or until tender.

5. Remove the beets from the heat and allow them to cool. Stir in the honey.

6. Serve hot or cold.

Nutrition Note: Beet greens are rich in potassium and an excellent source of carotenoids, flavonoid antioxidants, vitamin A and magnesium and are thought to have strong detoxification properties. Rather than throw them out, mix them into your salads. They taste great topped with a spoonful of pickled beets.

Shredded Carrot Salad

Make this salad to take to work for lunch, or serve as a dinner side dish with Almond and Herb Crusted Tilapia (page 97).

Prep time: 20 minutes

Makes: 4 servings

2 cups shredded carrots (about 8 ounces)

¼ cup Homemade Mayonnaise (page 248)

1½ teaspoons raw honey

1 teaspoon freshly chopped chives

½ teaspoon lemon thyme

2 teaspoons raw apple cider vinegar

2 tablespoons chopped walnuts

1. Combine all the ingredients in a bowl and stir well.

2. Refrigerate for at least an hour before serving.

PHASE 3 **Variation:** Once you reach Phase 3, you may add 2 tablespoons of fruit-juice sweetened, dried cranberries. They give the salad a sweet, tart taste that you are sure to enjoy.

Cook's Note: Lemon thyme is a type of thyme that has a lemon scent and taste. If it is not available, you can substitute regular fresh thyme.

Nutrition Note: Shredding or slicing vegetables increases nutrient availability.

Pickled Beets, page 80

Shredded Carrot Salad, page 81

Green Beans with Shiitake Mushrooms and Almonds, page 84

Stir-Fried Chinese Cabbage, Leeks and Pine Nuts, page 85

Green Beans with Shiitake Mushrooms and Almonds

Green beans and almonds are a classic combination. This side dish pairs perfectly with fish. Try it with Moroccan Spice-Rubbed Salmon (page 93) or Broiled Flounder with Herb Mayonnaise and Almonds (page 100).

Prep time: 15 minutes

Cook time: 10 minutes

Makes: 4 servings

½ **pound green beans**

2 **tablespoons extra virgin olive oil**

1 **shallot**

2 **cloves garlic**

4 **ounces shiitake mushrooms (caps only), sliced**

½ **teaspoon sea salt**

½ **teaspoon thyme leaves**

½ **teaspoon freshly chopped basil**

1 **teaspoon raw apple cider vinegar**

2 **tablespoons sliced almonds**

1. Steam the green beans for 5-6 minutes.
2. Heat a medium-sized frying pan over medium heat for about 1 minute, or until hot.
3. Add the oil and sauté the shallot and garlic for 1 minute, or until just limp.
4. Add the steamed green beans and the mushrooms and sauté for 2 minutes.
5. Stir in the salt, thyme, basil and vinegar and sauté for 1 minute.
6. Sprinkle on the almonds and serve immediately.

Cook's Note: Next time you are serving green beans, cook some extra and use the leftovers in this tasty, easy-to-make side dish. You can even use these beans as a salad topping.

Stir-Fried Chinese Cabbage, Leeks and Pine Nuts

If Chinese cabbage is not available, or if you prefer, you can substitute bok choy.

Prep time: 10 minutes

Cook time: about 8 minutes

. . . .

Makes: 4 servings

. . . .

3 tablespoons Ghee (page 234) or extra virgin olive oil, divided

2 leeks, white part only, cut into ¼-inch thick rounds and very well rinsed

1 clove garlic, crushed

1 head (1 pound) Chinese cabbage, cut horizontally into ½-inch slices

½ teaspoon sea salt

3 tablespoons pine nuts

1. Heat 1 tablespoon of the oil in a large frying pan over medium-high heat for 1 minute.

2. Add the leeks and sauté for 2 minutes, or until limp.

3. Add the garlic and sauté for 30 seconds.

4. Add the remaining oil and the cabbage, and stir fry for about 3 minutes, or until the cabbage is wilted.

5. Stir in the salt and pine nuts and stir fry for an additional minute.

PHASE 3 **Variation:** Once you reach Phase 3, you may add 1 tablespoon of tamari with the pine nuts, and stir fry for 1 minute.

Deviled Eggs

This old-time favorite has made a recent comeback. So if you haven't had it in a while, why not give it a try?

Prep time: 15 minutes

Makes: 12 pieces

6 eggs, hard boiled and peeled

3 tablespoons Herb Mayonnaise (page 248)

1 tablespoon mustard

¼ teaspoon sea salt

1. Cut the peeled, cooked eggs in half lengthwise. Remove the yolks to a small bowl and add the remaining ingredients. Break the yolks up with a fork and continue to mash until the mixture is smooth.

2. Spoon the filling back into the egg whites, or, if desired, pipe it back into the whites using a pastry bag fitted with a star tip.

Cook's Note: If you prefer, you can make this recipe into egg salad by mashing the whole cooked eggs, and combining them with the mayonnaise, mustard and salt. Serve over mixed greens.

Nutrition Note: Eggs are a healthy protein source with many dietary benefits. Eggs yolk are high in phosphatidylcholine, lutein, and zeaxanthin. Choose eggs that are labeled "USDA certified organic." The nutrients in eggs are essential to maintaining the healthy function of your heart, immune system, skin and even your brain.

Sautéed Carrots and Leeks

Sautéing vegetables brings out their natural sweetness. Try serving this simple recipe as an accompaniment to any poultry or fish dish.

Prep time: 20 minutes

Cook time: 10 minutes

. . . .

Makes: 2 cups

. . . .

2 tablespoons extra virgin olive oil

2 leeks, white part only, cleaned and cut into strips

1 clove garlic, crushed

3 carrots, peeled and julienned

½ teaspoon fresh thyme leaves

1 teaspoon freshly chopped parsley or cilantro

1 teaspoon freshly chopped basil

½ teaspoon sea salt

~~¼ teaspoon freshly ground black pepper~~

1. Heat the oil in a medium-sized frying pan over medium-high heat for 2 minutes, or until hot.

2. Sauté the leeks for 3 minutes, or until they start to brown.

3. Add the garlic and sauté for 30 seconds.

4. Add the carrots and sauté for about 5 minutes, or until tender.

5. Stir in the herbs, salt and pepper and sauté for 1 minute.

Nutrition Note: Carrots are one of the richest sources of the antioxidant beta carotene, which fights free radicals.

Artichoke Leek Soup

This recipe can be served as a smooth puree or a chunky vegetable soup. Either way, artichokes and leeks are an excellent combination.

Prep time: 15 minutes
Cook time: 25 minutes

Makes: 4 servings
(about 3½ cups)

1 tablespoon extra virgin olive oil

2 leeks, white part only, cut into 1-inch rounds and well rinsed

3 cloves garlic, chopped

1 can (14 ounces) artichoke hearts, chopped*

1½ cups Vegetable Stock (page 235)

½ cup Almond Milk (page 237)

½ teaspoon sea salt

1 teaspoon each freshly chopped parsley and oregano

1. Heat the oil in a 2-quart saucepot over medium heat for 2 minutes.

2. Sauté the leeks over medium heat for 3 minutes, or until they are limp and just starting to brown.

3. Add the garlic and sauté for 1 minute.

4. Add the remaining ingredients, and bring the soup to a boil over high heat. Lower to medium heat and simmer for 20 minutes.

5. Serve immediately.

* When available, thawed frozen artichoke hearts can be substituted for canned.

Cook's Note: An immersion blender is the ideal cooking tool for pureeing hot soup right in the saucepot. If you don't have an immersion blender, you can pour the hot soup into a food processor or blender. If you use a blender, be sure to remove the center cup from the lid, as built-up heat can cause the cover to blow off during blending.

Grilled Salmon over Assorted Greens with Fresh Herb Vinaigrette

Serve this healthy, delicious salmon salad for lunch or dinner any time of the year. You can broil the fish in the colder months, and grill it outdoors in the summer.

Prep time: 8 minutes

Cook time: 20 minutes

....

Makes: 2 servings

....

1 recipe Fresh Herb Vinaigrette (page 79)

Salmon
2 (6-ounce) salmon filets
1 teaspoon extra virgin olive oil
Sea salt
Freshly ground pepper

Greens
1 cup mixed greens, such as romaine and arugula
¼ cup shredded carrots
¼ cup chopped celery
¼ cup cooked string beans
2 tablespoons dried cranberries
2 asparagus spears, cooked and cut into 1-inch pieces
1 tablespoon toasted, chopped nuts, such as walnuts, almonds or pine nuts

1. Preheat the oven to Broil.
2. Prepare and set aside the Fresh Herb Vinaigrette.
3. Brush the salmon filets with the oil and season them with the salt and pepper.
4. Broil the filets for 8 minutes, or until the fish flakes easily with a fork.
5. While the fish is cooking, combine all of the ingredients for the mixed greens. Pour ½ the vinaigrette over the greens and toss well to coat.
6. Plate the greens and top each plate with a grilled filet. Drizzle the remaining vinaigrette over the fish, and serve immediately.

Cook's Note: Save yourself some time on future meals by preparing double the recipe of Fresh Herb Vinaigrette and broiling a couple of extra salmon filets to use for Sautéed Salmon Cakes (page 99).

Calico Slaw

This colorful slaw partners well with the fish recipes in this Phase. Prepare it in advance, and allow it to set in the refrigerator for at least a few hours, and preferably overnight, before serving.

Prep time: 20 minutes

Makes: about 6 cups

8 ounces white cabbage, shredded

8 ounces red cabbage, shredded

1 carrot, peeled and shredded

1 recipe (1 cup) Garlic-Shallot Mayonnaise (page 249)

1 teaspoon dry mustard

2 tablespoons raw apple cider vinegar

1 teaspoon sea salt

2½ teaspoons raw honey

½ teaspoon celery salt

1. Place the cabbage in a large bowl. Combine all the remaining ingredients and stir them into the cabbage. Mix until all the cabbage is coated.

2. Refrigerate for several hours or overnight before serving.

PHASE 2 **Variation:** Once you reach Phase 2, you may add fruit-juice sweetened, dried cranberries to this recipe. Their added sweetness is very appealing. You may also change the dry mustard to regular mustard, if desired.

Cook's Note: This recipe can be doubled, and will keep well in the refrigerator for several days.

Moroccan Spice-Rubbed Salmon

This blend of spices gives the salmon an Indian/Moroccan taste. The sautéed onions are optional, but highly recommended.

Prep time: 20 minutes

Cook time: 8 minutes

Makes: 2 servings

Rub
1 teaspoon garlic powder
½ teaspoon onion powder
½ teaspoon ground turmeric
¼ teaspoon sea salt
¼ teaspoon dried oregano
½ teaspoon garam masala or curry powder
⅛ teaspoon ground ginger

Fish
2 (6-ounce) salmon filets

Topping (not pictured)
1 small onion, sliced in rounds
1 tablespoon extra virgin olive oil

1. Preheat the oven to 450°F.

2. Combine all the ingredients for the rub.

3. Spread the rub on the flesh side of the salmon filets.

4. Cook the fish without turning for 8 minutes, or until the fish flakes easily with a fork.

5. While the fish is cooking, sauté the onion in the oil. Place the sautéed onion rounds on top of the fish for the last 2 minutes of cooking.

Cook's Note: If you have never used these spices, you might be hesitant about this recipe, but giving it a try might just open a whole new world of delicious possibilities to you and your family.

Stir-Fried Brown Rice and Vegetables

Brown rice has a nutty taste, and stir-frying gives it a little crunch and enhances the flavor. Adding chopped nuts and apricots ties all the flavors together for a satisfying, meatless meal.

Prep time: 20 minutes
Cook time: 8 minutes

Makes: 2 main dish servings

3 tablespoons extra virgin olive oil

4 scallions, chopped

2 cloves garlic, chopped

1 cup broccoli, broken into small florets or coarsely chopped

1 cup shredded carrots

1 cup sliced celery

1 cup cooked brown rice

½ teaspoon extra virgin olive oil

1 egg, lightly beaten

2 tablespoons chopped, toasted almonds or walnuts

2 tablespoons apricots or blueberries

1. Heat 2 tablespoons of the oil in a large frying pan over medium-high heat for about 2 minutes, or until hot.

2. Add the scallions, garlic, broccoli, carrots and celery and stir fry for 3 minutes, or until nicely browned.

3. Add the remaining 1 tablespoon of oil and the rice, and stir fry for another minute. Remove the rice and vegetables from the frying pan.

4. Add the ½ teaspoon of oil to the frying pan and heat for 30 seconds.

5. Pour the egg into the frying pan, making sure to cover the bottom of the pan. Cook for 1 minute, turn, and cook for 1 minute, or until set. Remove the egg and slice into thin strips.

6. Top the rice with the egg strips, and add the chopped nuts and apricots or blueberries. Serve immediately.

PHASE 3 **Variation:** Once you reach Phase 3, you may add 1 tablespoon of tamari at the same time as you add the rice. Continue as directed.

Apple Cider Vinegar and Honey Glazed Tilapia

A sweet and sour glaze sparks up this neutral-tasting fish.

Prep time: 10 minutes

Cook time: 8 minutes

....

Makes: 2 servings

....

2 (6-ounce) tilapia filets

1 tablespoon raw apple cider vinegar

1 tablespoon raw honey

1 teaspoon extra virgin olive oil

¼ teaspoon each sea salt, garlic and onion powder

½ teaspoon chopped parsley or cilantro

1 tablespoon chopped, roasted pine nuts or walnuts

1. Preheat the oven to Broil.

2. Place the filets on a baking sheet.

3. Combine the remaining ingredients, except for parsley or cilantro and nuts, and paint the top side of the filets with the glaze.

4. Cook the fish without turning for 8 minutes, or until it flakes easily with a fork.

5. Garnish with the chopped parsley or cilantro, and the nuts.

Cook's Note: Salmon can be substituted for tilapia if desired.

Almond and Herb Crusted Tilapia

The coating in this recipe, which replaces breadcrumbs, is one of many that you will find in the various Phases of this book. Best of all, these replacements add variety to your menus.

Prep time: 10 minutes
Cook time: 10-14 minutes

Makes: 4 servings

⅔ **cup Almond Meal (page 236)**

2 **teaspoons each freshly chopped parsley, thyme, oregano and chives**

1 **clove garlic, crushed**

½ **teaspoon sea salt**

4 **(4- to 6-ounce) tilapia filets**

3 **tablespoons coconut oil or Ghee (page 234)**

Herb Mayonnaise (page 248)

1. Combine the almond meal, herbs, garlic and salt on a dinner plate. Mix well.

2. Coat both sides of each filet with the mixture. Press the crumbs into the fish using your hands.

3. Place the fish on a small rack and let it sit in the refrigerator, uncovered, for at least 30 minutes, to allow the crumbs to dry and set in place.

4. Heat the oil or ghee in a frying pan over medium-high heat for about 3 minutes, or until hot.

5. Place the fish in the pan and cook for 5-7 minutes per side (depending on the thickness of the fish), until the crust is nicely browned.

6. Serve immediately, with Herb Mayonnaise.

Cook's Note: Breadcrumbs are generally made from white flour breads that are not permitted in this diet. This book provides a recipe for whole wheat breadcrumbs (Italian Breadcrumbs, page 244), but they are not permitted until Phase 4 of the diet. Almond meal blended with fresh herbs makes a delicious coating that is approved for Phase 1. You may never want to use breadcrumbs again!

Sautéed Salmon Cakes

In this recipe, chopped cooked brown rice takes the place of breadcrumbs, which are generally used as a binding agent. The rice adds a nutty flavor, as well as some crunch after it browns.

Prep time: 25 minutes
Standing time: 1 hour
Cook time: 12 minutes

Makes: 8 cakes

3 tablespoons extra virgin olive oil or Ghee (page 234), divided

1 small onion, chopped

1 clove garlic, crushed

1 carrot, finely chopped

1 stalk celery, finely chopped

2 shiitake mushrooms, finely chopped

2 teaspoons chopped parsley or cilantro

1 teaspoon chopped oregano

2 teaspoons chopped chives

½ teaspoon sea salt

1 egg, lightly beaten

¼ cup Homemade Mayonnaise (page 248)

1 teaspoon dry mustard

1½ cups cooked brown rice, chopped

½ pound cooked salmon, broken into large chunks

1. Heat 2 tablespoons of the oil or ghee in a medium-sized frying pan over medium-high heat for 2 minutes, or until hot.

2. Add the onion and sauté for 5 minutes, or until lightly browned.

3. Add the garlic, carrot, celery and mushrooms and sauté for 3 minutes, or until lightly browned.

4. Stir in the herbs and the salt. Remove the mixture to a bowl and allow it to cool for about 15 minutes.

5. Add the egg, mayonnaise, dry mustard and rice to the mixture, and mix well until they are incorporated.

6. Carefully stir in the salmon. Refrigerate the mixture for 30 minutes to allow it to set.

7. Line a plate or tray with waxed paper. Fill a ⅓-cup measuring cup with the mixture and turn out into your hand. Form the mixture into 8 cakes and place them on the paper-lined plate.

8. Cover the cakes and refrigerate for 30 minutes or for up to a day.

9. Heat the remaining tablespoon of oil in a large frying pan and sauté 4 salmon cakes at a time for about 3 minutes per side, or until nicely browned, adding additional olive oil if needed.

Cook's Note: The cakes can be frozen, either fully-cooked or before being cooked. Defrost and sauté raw cakes as directed. Fully-cooked cakes can be reheated in a 350°F oven for 10 minutes, or until hot. If you make 3-4 cups of brown rice at the beginning of Phase 1 and store it in the refrigerator, you will be ahead of the game, as there are several recipes that call for precooked brown rice.

Broiled Flounder with Herb Mayonnaise and Almonds

Topping fish with this creamy mayonnaise sauce keeps it moist.

Prep time: 15 minutes

Cook time: 10 minutes

. . . .

Makes: 4 servings

. . . .

1½ pounds flounder filet (4 large slices)

¼ teaspoon sea salt

½ cup Homemade Mayonnaise (page 248)

1 teaspoon dry mustard

2 tablespoons finely chopped shallots or scallions

1 clove garlic, crushed

½ teaspoon each freshly chopped oregano, thyme and basil

Chopped parsley for garnish

1. Preheat the oven to Broil.

2. Season the filets with the salt.

3. Combine the remaining ingredients, except for the parsley, and spread ½ the mixture over the fish. Reserve the remaining sauce for serving.

4. Broil the fish for about 10 minutes, until the mixture on top bubbles and is nicely browned, or until the fish is nicely browned and flakes easily with a fork.

5. Garnish with chopped parsley and serve immediately with the remaining mayonnaise sauce.

Cook's Note: Tilapia, sole or even salmon can be substituted for the flounder in this recipe. If a thicker fish is used, broil for 2 additional minutes.

Sautéed Filet of Sole with Artichoke Pesto

Try this unique pesto on your fish. For a snack, use any extra sauce as a dip for celery and carrots.

Prep time: 10 minutes

Cook time: 10 minutes

....

Makes: 1½ cups pesto and 4 servings fish with pesto

....

Pesto

1 tablespoon extra virgin olive oil or coconut oil

1 small shallot, chopped

1 clove garlic, chopped

8 almonds

1 can (14 ounces) artichoke hearts, drained

½ teaspoon sea salt

¼ cup basil leaves

2 tablespoons parsley leaves, stems removed

¼ cup Homemade Mayonnaise (page 248)

Fish

1 tablespoon extra virgin olive oil

½ teaspoon garlic powder

½ teaspoon onion powder

¼ teaspoon sea salt

4 filets of sole

1. Heat the oil in a small frying pan over medium-high heat for 2 minutes, or until hot.

2. Add the shallots and garlic and sauté for 1 minute, or until limp.

3. Place the almonds, artichoke hearts, salt, basil, parsley and mayonnaise in the bowl of a food processor. Cover, and pulse several times until you reach the desired consistency - the pesto can be served chunky or smooth, to your taste.

4. Heat the oil in a medium-sized frying pan over medium heat for 1 minute, or until hot.

5. Combine the garlic powder, onion powder and salt.

6. Place 2 filets in the frying pan. Sprinkle the tops of the filets with the garlic salt mixture and cook the fish for 2 minutes. Carefully turn the fish, sprinkle with more of the garlic salt mixture, and cook for 2 minutes. Remove the cooked filets to a platter.

7. Repeat Step 6 with the remaining filets.

8. Serve each filet topped with 2-3 tablespoons of the pesto.

9. Store any remaining pesto in the refrigerator, for future use as a dip with carrots and celery.

....

PHASE 3 **Variation:** Once you reach Phase 3, you may add ¼ cup grated Parmesan cheese to this pesto before serving. Try it over buckwheat pasta, topped with additional grated cheese and freshly chopped tomatoes.

....

Nutty Coconut Delight

This recipe is a real treat. During Phase 1 of this diet, you are urged to keep your intake of sweets to a minimum, so restrict yourself to one. Be forewarned, however, that once you taste these treats, stopping at one might be easier said than done!

Prep time: 10 minutes

Cook time: 15 minutes

Set up time: several hours

Makes: 15 (2-inch) balls

¼ cup Ghee (page 234)

½ cup raw honey

½ cup almonds

1 teaspoon cinnamon

¾ cup unsweetened coconut

½ cup walnuts, chopped

1. Preheat the oven to 350°F.

2. Place the ghee, honey, almonds and cinnamon in the bowl of a food processor fitted with a steel blade. Pulse 6 or 7 times, or until the nuts are ground.

3. Grease the bottom of an 8-inch square baking pan. Spread the nut and honey mixture over the bottom of the greased pan.

4. Sprinkle the coconut over the honey nut mixture, and then sprinkle the chopped walnuts over the coconut.

5. Place the pan in the oven and bake for 15-20 minutes, or until the edges bubble and begin to brown.

6. Allow the pan to cool and then refrigerate it for several hours or overnight.

7. Scoop the mixture into balls using a small ice cream scoop or serving spoon.

8. Serve immediately and refrigerate any leftovers.

Cook's Note: Store in a sealed container in the refrigerator, or freeze them and defrost later for a take-along snack. Of course, everyone in your family will love these treats so much, you might not have many leftovers to freeze.

Acai and Blueberry Spritzer

This cool spritzer is tasty and nutritious. Have it any time of day for a great pick-me-up.

Prep time: 5 minutes

Makes: 1 drink

3 ounces unsweetened acai juice

3 ounces unsweetened blueberry juice

1 teaspoon raw honey

2 ounces sparkling water

1. Combine the juices and the honey and pour into a tall, ice-filled glass.

2. Top with the sparkling water and stir.

Nutrition Note: The acai berry is native to Brazil. It is rich in anthocyanins and flavonoids – powerful antioxidants that play a role in the body's cell protection system. Eating a diet rich in antioxidants may help reduce the effects of disease and aging by neutralizing free radicals, which are harmful by-products produced by the body. The darker blue or purple the fruit, the higher it is in antioxidants, so this acai and blueberry combo is a real nutritional winner.

Coconut Almond Custard

If you have never made custard and think that it is beyond your skill level, you will be pleasantly surprised by just how easy this recipe is to make.

Prep time: 15 minutes

Cook time: 1 hour and 30-40 minutes

Makes: 4 servings

2 eggs

1 cup Coconut Milk (page 237)

1 tablespoon ~~agave nectar~~ *raw honey*

1 teaspoon vanilla

⅛ teaspoon almond extract

⅛ teaspoon sea salt

½ cup unsweetened coconut

Toasted coconut (see Cook's Note) **and chopped almonds for topping**

1. Preheat the oven to 350ºF.

2. Combine all of the ingredients, except for the coconut, in a mixing bowl. Using a wire whisk or electric hand mixer, whisk or beat for 1 minute, or until the egg white is thoroughly combined with the other ingredients.

3. Stir in the coconut.

4. Pour ½ cup of the mixture into each of four 6-ounce custard cups or heat-proof bowls. Place the filled cups in a baking dish. Fill the baking dish with enough hot water to reach about ⅓ of the way up the sides of the cups, being careful not to get any water into the cups.

5. Bake in the preheated oven for ~~1 hour and 30-40~~ **40-50** minutes, or until the custard is set and a knife inserted about an inch from a cup's center comes out clean.

6. Carefully remove the custards from the water and allow them to cool for at least 30 minutes before serving, or refrigerate and serve chilled.

7. Sprinkle with toasted coconut and chopped almonds before serving.

Cook's Note: To toast the coconut for the topping, spread ½ cup of unsweetened coconut in a thin layer on a baking tray. Place the tray in the preheated oven before you begin preparing the custards, and bake for 5 minutes, or until the coconut is lightly browned. Keep a close eye on it, as coconut toasts very quickly. Allow the coconut to cool, and store any unused portion in an airtight container for later use.

Phase 2
Contents

Phase 2: The Early Reentry Phase *(three weeks)*

Phase 2 of the Lyme Inflammation Diet® is to be followed for three weeks after the conclusion of Phase 1. During Phase 2, your goal is to slowly reintroduce healthy foods that have a low risk of triggering inflammation. You will do this by gradually adding each food group's new foods to your diet. For example, try adding each group's new foods every other day: on day one, add the new fruits; on day three, add the new nuts; and so forth.

It is vitally important that you do not rush the reintroduction of foods. If you experience any symptoms of inflammation after the foods are reintroduced, this is a sign that you should continue to avoid them for the time being (the foods that carry the highest risk of triggering inflammation are nuts and certain fruits, such as mangos).

Shredded Carrot Salad, page 81

Foods Allowed During Phase 2

Beverages
Green tea
Vegetable juice[1]
Carbonated water,
  such as Perrier

Fruits[2]
Apricot
Cantaloupe
Date
Fig
Mango
Olives NEW
Pear
Pineapple
Plum NEW
Prune
Watermelon

Nuts and Seeds
Brazil nuts
Cashews
Pecans
Pumpkin seeds
Sesame seeds
Sunflower seeds

Vegetables
Arame [3] NEW
Dulse [3] NEW
Fennel NEW
Hijiki [3] NEW
Kelp [3] NEW
Kombu [3] NEW
Nori [3] NEW
Pumpkin
Squash
Sweet potato
Tapioca (cassava)
Wakame [3] NEW
Wasabi NEW

Grains
Brown rice flour NEW
Oat flour NEW
Oatmeal

Beans and Legumes
Black beans
Chickpeas
Kidney beans
Lentils
Navy beans
Peas
Pinto beans

Protein
Lamb
Venison NEW
White meat chicken NEW
White meat turkey NEW

Herb and Spices
Black pepper

Fats
Margarines without
  trans fats [3]

Sweeteners [2]
Agave nectar
Honey[5,6] NEW
Maple syrup
Sorbitol
Xylitol

Other
Coconut kefir[6,7]

[1] Make sure it does not contain tomato, which is not permitted until Phase 3.

[2] Use sparingly, as they are very high in sugar.

[3] These are all sea vegetables. If you are unfamiliar with them, see page 59 for more information.

[4] Examples include Earth Balance, Smart Balance and Benechol.

[5] If you are unsure about the difference between honey and raw honey, see page 57.

[6] For more information on where to purchase, see the Resources section (page 274).

[7] See page 60 for definition and health benefits.

Blueberry Oatmeal Pancakes

This recipe contains a trifecta of "good for you" foods. Blueberries are the number one fruit for antioxidants, and oats and almonds are heart-healthy and may help lower cholesterol. Most importantly, though, these pancakes are delectable!

Prep time: 15 minutes

Cook time: 6-18 minutes

Makes: about 8 (4-inch) pancakes

¾ cup old fashioned oats

1 cup Almond Milk (page 237)

¾ cup oat flour

1 teaspoon cream of tartar

½ teaspoon baking soda

¼ teaspoon sea salt

1 egg, separated

2 tablespoons Ghee (page 234) or extra virgin olive oil

1 cup blueberries

1. Preheat a frying pan or griddle (nonstick preferred).

2. Combine the oats and almond milk in a small bowl, and allow to stand for at least 5 minutes to soften.

3. Meanwhile, combine the flour, cream of tartar, baking soda and salt in a medium-sized bowl.

4. Combine the egg yolk and the ghee or oil, and stir into the softened oatmeal.

5. Add the oatmeal mixture to the flour mixture and stir well to combine.

6. Using an electric mixer, beat the egg whites until they form soft peaks. Fold the beaten egg whites into the mixture.

7. Before making the first pancake, wipe the hot pan or griddle with a folded paper towel soaked in a small amount of ghee or extra virgin olive oil.

8. Measure ⅓ cup of batter per pancake, and pour onto the griddle.

9. Scatter blueberries on the top of each pancake, and cook for about 3 minutes. The pancake is ready to turn when bubbles form on the surface, and the edges begin to set. Turn the pancakes, and cook for 2-3 minutes.

Cook's Note: Correct timing and griddle temperature may vary, as cooktops and stoves vary so widely that it is difficult to give precise instructions. Cook these pancakes as you cook any other pancake recipe. Just make certain that the cooking surface is hot enough before you pour the batter, because otherwise, the pancakes will stick. If the surface is too hot, however, the pancakes will brown too quickly while remaining raw in the center. Jot down the timing and temperature that work for you in the margin of this recipe, so that the next time you make these pancakes, you will have the information at hand.

Carrot Pineapple Muffins

These muffins taste like little carrot cakes. Eat them for breakfast, for an afternoon snack or even for dessert.

Prep time: 30 minutes

Cook time: 15-20 minutes

. . . .

Makes: 6 muffins

. . . .

¾ cup old fashioned oats

⅓ cup Almond Milk (page 237)

⅓ cup oat flour

1 tablespoon Homemade Baking Powder (page 238)

1 teaspoon ground cinnamon

½ teaspoon ground or freshly grated ginger

¼ teaspoon sea salt

3 tablespoons agave nectar

1 egg, lightly beaten

2 tablespoons extra virgin olive oil or Ghee (page 234)

1 teaspoon vanilla

1 cup shredded carrots

½ cup fresh pineapple, chopped

⅓ cup chopped walnuts

1. Preheat the oven to 400°F.

2. Place the oats in a medium-sized bowl. Pour in the almond milk and stir well. Allow the oatmeal to stand and soften while you assemble the remaining ingredients.

3. In a small bowl, combine the flour, baking powder, cinnamon, ginger and salt, and set aside.

4. Combine the agave nectar, egg, ghee or oil and vanilla, and stir into the standing oatmeal.

5. Stir the flour mixture into the oatmeal mixture, and stir well to combine.

6. Stir in the carrots, pineapple and walnuts.

7. Spray a 6-cup muffin pan with non-stick olive oil cooking spray. Using a ⅓-cup measuring cup, fill the muffin cups almost to the top with the mixture.

8. Bake in the preheated oven for 15-20 minutes, or until a toothpick inserted in the center of a muffin comes out clean.

Cook's Note: These muffins can be made into a breakfast bread. Using an 8-inch loaf pan, bake the bread at 350°F for 40 minutes, or until a toothpick inserted in the center comes out clean.

Overnight Oatmeal with Dried Fruit and Almonds

This nutritious breakfast will start your day off right.

Prep time: 15 minutes

Cook time: 8 hours

. . . .

Makes: 4 (1 cup) servings

. . . .

1 cup steel-cut oats

2½ cups Almond Milk (page 237)

2½ cups Coconut Milk (page 237)

1 cup water

¼ teaspoon sea salt

2 tablespoons maple syrup

½ teaspoon vanilla extract

1½ teaspoons ground cinnamon

½ teaspoon ground ginger

¼ teaspoon nutmeg

1 cup chopped, mixed, unsweetened, dried fruits, such as apricots, cranberries, cherries, blueberries or figs

2 tablespoons sliced almonds or chopped pistachio nuts

Additional Almond Milk (page 237)

Additional cinnamon

1. Place all the ingredients, except for the nuts, additional almond milk and additional cinnamon, in the bowl of a slow cooker. Cover the cooker, and set it to cook on Low for 8 hours.

2. Spoon the oatmeal into bowls, and top with the nuts, additional almond milk and/or additional cinnamon if desired.

3. Refrigerate any leftovers, which can be reheated.

Cook's Note: Turn on the slow cooker, as directed in Step 2, just before you go to bed at night. The next morning, everyone will wake up to a delicious bowl of oatmeal, no matter what time they leave for their day of work or school.

Granola

This granola can be eaten as a breakfast cereal with almond or coconut milk, or as a snack anytime.

Prep time: 15 minutes

Cook time: 30-40 minutes

Makes: about 7 cups

2½ cups old fashioned oats

1 cup unsweetened coconut

1 tablespoon ground flaxseed

1 cup chopped pecans

½ cup sunflower seeds

1 cup ~~shelled pistachio nuts or~~ sliced almonds

2 teaspoons cinnamon

⅓ cup maple syrup

⅓ cup Ghee (page 234)

1 teaspoon vanilla extract

½ cup fruit-juice sweetened, dried cranberries

½ cup chopped dried apricots

1. Preheat the oven to 350°F.

2. Combine the oats, coconut, flaxseed, pecans, sunflower seeds, pistachios (or almonds) and cinnamon on a large baking sheet.

3. Combine the syrup, oil and vanilla in a measuring cup.

4. Pour the syrup mixture over the oats and nuts, and toss well to coat.

5. Bake for 30-40 minutes, or until lightly browned.

6. Remove the granola from the oven and add the dried fruit.

7. Allow to cool completely before storing in an air-tight container.

Cook's Note: When you reach the later Phases of the diet, you may add different fruits and nuts where permitted, such as raisins in Phase 4.

Oat Crepes

Top these crepes with Berry Pear Sauce (page 256) or Blueberry or Raspberry Syrup (page 255). For an extra special treat, fill the crepes with Blueberry Coconut Ice Cream (page 150), freeze them, and then serve with Blueberry Syrup.

Prep time: 15 minutes

Cook time: 30 minutes

Makes: about 12 crepes

2 eggs, well beaten

1 cup oat flour

1 cup Almond Milk (page 237) or oat milk

2 tablespoons Ghee (page 234) or extra virgin olive oil

⅛ teaspoon sea salt

1 teaspoon vanilla

1. Combine all the ingredients in a large mixing bowl. Mix well with a wire whisk or electric mixer until the batter is smooth.

2. Preheat an 8- or 9-inch frying pan or crepe pan until water sprinkled on the pan sizzles.

3. Before making the first crepe, wipe the hot pan with a folded paper towel soaked in oil.

4. Fill a ladle with 3 tablespoons of batter, or use a not-quite-filled ¼-cup measuring cup. Pour the batter into the pan, quickly tilting the pan to spread the batter over the bottom. Allow the crepe to cook for about 1½ minutes, or until it is set and lightly browned. Using a nonstick spatula, turn the crepe and cook 1½ minutes.

5. Remove the crepe to a plate and cover with a piece of waxed paper.

6. Continue cooking as directed, placing a piece of waxed paper between each cooked crepe, until all are cooked.

7. Use in any recipe calling for crepes, or serve immediately with Berry Pear Sauce if desired.

Cook's Note: There's a knack to making crepes, and it takes some practice to learn to make them perfectly every time. Here are two suggestions for success: first and most importantly, make sure the pan is the correct temperature. Heat the pan over medium-high heat for 3-5 minutes. If a drop of water sizzles in the pan, it is at the right temperature. Also, crepes should be thin, so after pouring the batter, remove the pan from the heat and tilt it in all directions to spread the batter over the bottom of the pan. If you follow these two guidelines, you will be much less likely to have problems with your crepes.

Indian Chickpea and Spinach Fritters

The curry in these fritters gives them a decidedly Indian flavor. If you don't like Indian food, take a chance and try this recipe anyway – you might be pleasantly surprised. Many of our taste testers who "don't like Indian food" ended up asking for the recipe!

Prep time: 20 minutes

Cook time: 10 minutes

....

Makes: 8 fritters

....

½ cup brown rice flour

½ teaspoon baking soda

¼ teaspoon cream of tartar

¼ teaspoon freshly ground black pepper

½ teaspoon sea salt

1 egg

¼ cup water

1 cup chickpeas, drained, rinsed and coarsely chopped

3 cups fresh baby spinach, finely chopped

½ small onion, chopped

1 clove garlic, crushed

2 teaspoons curry powder

2 teaspoons sesame seeds

1 teaspoon chopped oregano

1-3 tablespoons Ghee (page 234) or extra virgin olive oil, divided

1. Preheat the oven to 225°F.

2. Combine the flour, baking soda, cream of tartar, pepper and salt in a large bowl.

3. Combine the egg and water and whisk until smooth. Add it to the flour and stir until smooth.

4. Add all the remaining ingredients, except for the ghee or oil, and stir well to combine.

5. Heat 1 tablespoon of the ghee or oil in a medium-sized frying pan over medium-high heat for 3 minutes, or until hot.

6. Using a standard ice cream scoop, drop the mixture into the hot pan. Press each fritter flat to form a 3-inch circle.

7. Cook 4 fritters at a time for 2½ minutes per side, or until nicely browned.

8. Remove the cooked fritters to a baking sheet and keep them warm in the preheated oven while you prepare the remaining fritters, adding the additional tablespoons of oil if needed.

Cook's Note: If you have a large enough frying pan, you can cook all the fritters at once. In that case, you need not preheat the oven.

Chicken Salad

This is a quick lunch if you have all the ingredients prepared in advance. Be sure to make the sauces and condiments for each Phase that are found in the Sauces and Condiments section, so that you will have what you need to prepare the recipes at a moment's notice.

Prep time: 10 minutes

Makes: 4 servings
(about 3 cups)

2 cups cooked white meat chicken, cut into ½-inch chunks

½ cup chopped celery

½ cup fruit-juice sweetened, dried cranberries

½ cup cashews

¼ cup chopped dried apricots

½ teaspoon sea salt

½ teaspoon garlic powder

¼ teaspoon freshly ground black pepper

1 teaspoon lemon juice

1 cup Herb Mayonnaise (page 248)

1. Combine all the ingredients in a medium-sized bowl and stir well, coating everything with the mayonnaise.

2. Refrigerate the salad for at least 30 minutes, or overnight, before serving.

3. Serve over mixed greens.

Cook's Note: The flavors in this chicken salad blend and taste better when it's refrigerated for a while, so make this recipe ahead of time whenever possible.

Spinach and Lentil Salad with Warm Honey Vinegar Dressing

This easy-to-make salad looks and tastes like a restaurant-quality dish. Your family and friends will be impressed.

Prep time: 15 minutes
Cook time: 45 minutes

Makes: 2 servings

½ cup lentils

2 tablespoons extra virgin olive oil

1 medium onion, cut into quarters and then sliced into strips

2 cloves garlic, crushed

3 tablespoons raw apple cider vinegar

1 tablespoon honey

¼ cup extra virgin olive oil

2 cups baby spinach leaves

2 hard cooked eggs, sliced

10 toasted pecans

½ ripe avocado, sliced

1. Cook the lentils according to the package directions.

2. While the lentils are cooking, heat the oil in a small frying pan over medium-high heat for about 2 minutes, or until hot.

3. Sauté the onion for about 5 minutes, or until golden-brown.

4. Add the garlic and cook for 1 minute.

5. Combine the vinegar and honey, and pour it over the onions in the pan. Stir well to combine, and cook for 30 seconds.

6. Add the remaining ¼ cup of oil to the pan and cook for 30 seconds.

7. Divide the spinach between two bowls. Top each with half of the onion vinaigrette mixture and toss well.

8. Spoon the cooked lentils over the salads. Top with a splash of the dressing, and the eggs, nuts and avocado.

Cook's Note: Cook the lentils and eggs in advance. Then, all that is left to do is to make the dressing. Reheat the lentils and eggs (before slicing), and then assemble the salad.

Salted Roasted Chickpeas

Grab a handful of this tasty, healthy snack whenever you have a craving for something salty and nutty.

Prep time: 5 minutes

Cook time: 35-45 minutes

....

Makes: about 1¼ cups

....

1 can (14 ounces) organic chickpeas, drained and rinsed

½ tablespoon extra virgin olive oil

¼ teaspoon garlic powder

½ teaspoon sea salt

⅛ teaspoon freshly ground black pepper

1. Preheat the oven to 450°F.
2. Pour the rinsed chickpeas onto a paper towel and blot dry.
3. Place the chickpeas on a baking sheet. Pour the oil over the chickpeas and toss well to coat them all.
4. Combine the garlic powder, salt and pepper and sprinkle over the chickpeas.
5. Roast in the preheated oven for 35-45 minutes, or until browned and crunchy. Turn the chickpeas with a large spoon or spatula once or twice during cooking to ensure even roasting.

Cook's Note: Keep an eye on the chickpeas during the last few minutes of roasting, to make sure they do not burn. They should be crunchy as soon as you remove them from the oven; if they are still soft, they need more time.

Curried Cashews

Nuts are a great snack. In this recipe, the curry adds an Indian spice.

Prep time: 5 minutes

Cook time: 10 minutes

....

Makes: 2 cups

....

2 tablespoons Ghee (page 234)

1 tablespoon curry powder, divided

½-1 teaspoon sea salt

2 cups roasted cashew nuts

¼ teaspoon garlic powder

1. Preheat the oven to 350°F.
2. Heat the ghee in a small frying pan over medium-high heat for 1 minute, or until it bubbles.
3. Combine the curry and salt and add half of this mixture to the frying pan. Cook for 30 seconds.
4. Toss the cashews in the curry butter, and then spread them in a single layer on a baking sheet.
5. Bake for 10 minutes, or until the nuts are shiny and hot. Remove from the oven.
6. Add the garlic powder to the remaining curry salt mixture, and sprinkle it over the warm nuts.
7. Cool completely before serving.

Apple and Pear Salad with Honey Mustard Dressing

Boston lettuce is strangely under used in salads. Its soft, almost buttery leaf works especially well with the fruits in this recipe.

Prep time: 15 minutes

Makes: 2 servings
(½ cup dressing)

Salad
2 large Boston lettuce leaves

1 green apple, peeled and sliced

1 medium pear, peeled and sliced

2 tablespoons fruit-juice sweetened, dried cranberries or cherries

½ cup pecans

Dressing
1 tablespoon mustard

2 tablespoons raw apple cider vinegar

1 tablespoon raw honey

½ tablespoon maple syrup

¼ teaspoon sea salt

⅛ teaspoon freshly ground black pepper

⅛ teaspoon each garlic powder and onion powder

¼ cup extra virgin olive oil

1. Place the lettuce leaves on two salad plates.
2. Top with the fruits and nuts.
3. Combine the dressing ingredients in the order given, whisking in the olive oil until the dressing forms an emulsion.
4. Spoon 2 tablespoons of dressing over the salads just before serving. Refrigerate any leftover dressing.

Cook's Note: This salad can be turned into a main dish by topping it with broiled fish or chicken.

Lentil Soup

Make this soup and freeze half of it for a busy day when you have no time to cook. It is hardy enough for dinner, but can also be taken to work, to have for lunch after a quick reheat.

Prep time: 25 minutes
Cook time: 50 minutes

Makes: about 1½ quarts

2 tablespoons extra virgin olive oil

1 large onion, chopped

4 cloves garlic, chopped

2 carrots, peeled and chopped

3 stalks celery, chopped

1 cup (2 ounces) chopped spinach

1 teaspoon sea salt

½ teaspoon freshly ground black pepper

1 tablespoon chopped chives

1 teaspoon chopped parley

1 teaspoon chopped thyme

½ teaspoon chopped rosemary

6 cups Vegetable Stock (page 235)

½ pound lentils, rinsed

1. Heat 2 tablespoons of the oil in a large saucepan over medium-high heat for about 2 minutes, or until hot.

2. Add the onion and garlic and sauté for about 6 minutes, or until lightly browned.

3. Add the carrots, celery, spinach, salt, pepper and herbs and continue to sauté until the vegetables are limp.

4. Add the stock, and stir in the lentils.

5. Bring the soup to a boil. Reduce the heat and simmer for 40 minutes, or until the lentils are tender.

6. Adjust the seasoning to taste, and serve.

PHASE 3 **Variation:** Once you reach Phase 3, add a 14-ounce can of diced tomatoes with herbs at the same time as you add the broth. The tomatoes will add even more flavor to this hardy soup.

Cook's Note: This soup will thicken as it stands because the lentils continue to soak up the liquid. If the soup becomes too thick, you can add some extra Vegetable Stock or water and simmer for a few additional minutes.

Nutrition Note: Lentils, while small in size, are big in nutrients! They are a good source of B-vitamins and minerals, including, but not limited to, iron. They are among the healthiest sources of plant-based protein and are very high in dietary fiber, yet low in fat.

Autumn Mixed Green and Roasted Butternut Squash Salad

Prep time: 15 minutes

Cook time: 40 minutes

....

Makes: 2 servings

....

Butternut Squash

8 ounces butternut squash, cut into ½-inch cubes

2 tablespoons extra virgin olive oil

1 tablespoon maple syrup

½ teaspoon onion powder

½ teaspoon garlic powder

½ teaspoon sea salt

¼ teaspoon freshly ground black pepper

Dressing

2 tablespoons acai, raspberry or pomegranate juice

1 tablespoon mustard

1 tablespoon raw apple cider vinegar

1 tablespoon raw honey

2 teaspoons maple syrup

¼ teaspoon sea salt

⅛ teaspoon garlic powder

⅛ teaspoon onion powder

⅛ teaspoon freshly ground black pepper

¼ cup extra virgin olive oil

Salad

2 cups mixed greens

2 tablespoons toasted pine nuts or walnuts

2 tablespoons fruit-juice sweetened, dried cranberries

1. Preheat the oven to 425°F.

2. Place the squash on a baking sheet in a single layer.

3. Combine the oil, syrup, onion and garlic powder, and salt and pepper and pour the mixture over the squash. Toss well to coat.

4. Roast the squash for 30-40 minutes, or until the pieces start to caramelize.

5. Meanwhile, combine the dressing ingredients in the order given, whisking in the olive oil until the dressing forms an emulsion.

6. Place the greens on two salad plates and top with the roasted squash, nuts and cranberries.

7. Spoon 2 tablespoons of dressing over each salad and serve immediately.

Mixed Fruit and Green Salad with Blueberry Dressing

Berries, cherries and greens combine to make this colorful and scrumptious salad. The blueberry dressing intensifies the fruit flavors.

Prep time: 15 minutes

Makes: 1 serving

Salad
1 cup mixed greens, such as romaine, arugula and napa cabbage
¼ cup sliced carrots
½ small cucumber, sliced
½ teaspoon each freshly chopped parsley and basil
⅓ cup mixed fruits, such as blueberries, cherries and raspberries
2 tablespoons cashews or walnuts

Blueberry Dressing
2 tablespoons blueberry juice
½ tablespoon raw apple cider vinegar
½ tablespoon extra virgin olive oil
¼ teaspoon mustard
¼ teaspoon raw honey
⅛ teaspoon sea salt

1. Combine the salad ingredients in a bowl.
2. Whisk together the dressing ingredients and pour over the salad.
3. Serve immediately.

Cook's Note: Use pine nuts or walnuts in Phase 1 of this diet. Once you reach Phase 2, cashews are permitted and may be substituted. Use this recipe as a template, and substitute any permitted nuts and fruits you like to add variety to your diet.

Artichoke Hummus

Hummus has become a very popular food. Chickpeas are usually the star of the show, but in this recipe they share the stage with artichoke hearts.

Prep time: 15 minutes

Makes: 2 cups

1 can (15.5 ounces) chickpeas, drained, with 2 tablespoons liquid set aside

1 can (14 ounces) artichoke hearts, drained

1 teaspoon sesame oil

3 tablespoons extra virgin olive oil

1 clove garlic

1 tablespoon raw apple cider vinegar

1 sprig parsley, leaves only

4 basil leaves

1 sprig oregano, leaves only

½ teaspoon sea salt

¼ teaspoon freshly ground black pepper

½ teaspoon each garlic and onion powder

1. Combine all the ingredients in the bowl of a food processor. Pulse several times to chop, and then turn on and process continually until the hummus is a smooth consistency.

2. If the hummus is too thick, add 1 tablespoon at a time of chickpea liquid until you reach the desired consistency.

3. Serve as a dip with carrot and celery sticks.

Nutrition Note: Artichokes and chickpeas are good sources of fiber and rich in folates and vitamins A and B6. They are a winning flavor and nutrition combination.

Chickpea and Sweet Potato Patties

Chickpeas and sweet potatoes combine beautifully in these satisfying patties. Serve them over greens for lunch, or as a side dish with dinner.

Prep time: 10 minutes
Cook time: 6 minutes

Makes: 5 patties

1 cup (8 ounces) cooked sweet potato, mashed

1 cup chickpeas, chopped

1 clove garlic, crushed

4 scallions, white part only, chopped

¼ teaspoon sea salt

⅛ teaspoon freshly ground black pepper

2 tablespoons Homemade Mayonnaise (page 248)

½ tablespoon mustard

1 teaspoon paprika

1 teaspoon each freshly chopped parsley, oregano and basil

⅔ cup Almond Meal (page 236)

2 tablespoons Ghee (page 234) or extra virgin olive oil

1. Combine all the ingredients, except for the almond meal and oil, and mix well.

2. Form the mixture into 5 patties (about ⅓ cup each).

3. Dredge the patties in the almond meal and refrigerate them for at least 30 minutes.

4. Heat the oil in a small frying pan over medium-high heat for 3 minutes, or until hot.

5. Cook the patties in the hot oil for 2-3 minutes per side, or until nicely browned.

Cook's Note: These patties reheat well in a toaster oven or frying pan. They can also be frozen and reheated any time you need a quick meal.

Sweet and Tangy Baked Chicken

This chicken, with its dark, tangy sauce and moist, tender meat, is finger-licking good!

Prep time: 15 minutes

Cook time: 50 minutes

....

Makes: 4 servings

....

2 tablespoons extra virgin olive oil

1 medium onion, chopped

4 large garlic cloves, peeled

2 large (12 ounces each) chicken breasts with skin and bones, cut in half

½ teaspoon sea salt

¼ teaspoon freshly ground black pepper

2 sprigs rosemary

2 sprigs thyme

2 tablespoons honey

3 tablespoons raw apple cider vinegar

3 tablespoons water or Chicken Stock (page 240)

1 tablespoon mustard

½-1 cup water

1. Preheat the oven to 400ºF.

2. Heat the oil in a heavy-bottomed frying pan (cast iron preferred) over medium-high heat for about 2 minutes.

3. Add the onion and sauté for 2 minutes.

4. Add the garlic and sauté for 1 minute.

5. Remove the onion and garlic from the pan and reserve for later use.

6. Season the skin of the chicken with salt and pepper and add the chicken to the hot pan, skin side down. Cook for 3 minutes, or until browned. Then, turn the chicken and cook for 3 minutes.

7. Add the rosemary and thyme to the pan.

8. Combine the honey, vinegar, water or stock and mustard, and stir the mixture into the chicken.

9. Return the onions and garlic to the pan and stir well.

10. Place the pan in the preheated oven and cook for 30 minutes. After 30 minutes, check to see if the sauce has become too thick and syrupy; if it has, stir in the remaining ½-1 cup water.

11. Turn the chicken breasts and cook for 15 minutes, or until the chicken is nicely browned.

12. Remove the rosemary and thyme sprigs. If the sauce is still too thick, stir in a little more water.

13. Place the chicken on a serving platter, and top with the sauce.

Cook's Note: If your family prefers dark meat chicken to white, wait until Phase 3 to make this recipe.

Veggie Burgers

Serve these veggie burgers on beds of Boston lettuce.

Prep time: 25 minutes

Cook time: 10 minutes

. . . .

Makes: 2-3 burgers

. . . .

2 tablespoons extra virgin olive oil

¼ cup finely chopped onions

1 clove garlic

1 cup cooked brown rice

3 tablespoons finely chopped chickpeas or kidney beans, or Artichoke Hummus (page 126)

2 tablespoons finely chopped pecans or sunflower seeds

1 teaspoon ground flaxseed

¼ cup chopped shiitake mushroom caps

¼ cup shredded carrot

¼ cup shredded zucchini, with liquid squeezed out

1 teaspoon mustard

2 teaspoons Herb Mayonnaise (page 248)

1 teaspoon freshly chopped cilantro or parsley

1 egg, slightly beaten

½ teaspoon sea salt

½ teaspoon celery salt

1. Heat 1 tablespoon of the oil in a medium-sized frying pan over medium heat for 3 minutes, or until hot.

2. Sauté the onions for 3 minutes, or until lightly browned.

3. Add the garlic and sauté for 30 seconds.

4. Remove the onions and garlic from the pan and allow them to cool slightly.

5. Meanwhile, combine all the rice and the remaining ingredients in a mixing bowl. Add the cooled onions and garlic.

6. Drain any liquid that might have accumulated in the mixing bowl from the zucchini.

7. Mix well, and form into 2 large or 3 medium-sized patties.

8. Cover and refrigerate the patties for at least 30 minutes.

9. Heat the remaining tablespoon of oil in the frying pan for 2 minutes, or until hot.

10. Cook the patties for about 5 minutes per side, or until nicely browned.

11. Serve topped with Herb Mayonnaise (page 248) or Garlic-Shallot Mayonnaise (page 249).

Cook's Note: These patties are very moist. Allowing them to stand uncovered in the refrigerator for 30 minutes or longer will ensure that they do not come apart when cooked.

Sesame Chicken Tenders

Puffed millet is usually eaten as a breakfast cereal, but in this recipe, it is ground in a coffee grinder and mixed with seasoning and toasted sesame seeds. This mixture makes an outstanding breading for chicken tenders that you and your family will love.

Prep time: 10 minutes
Cook time: 15-20 minutes

Makes: 4 servings

½ cup ground ~~puffed millet~~ *sesame seed*
1 teaspoon garlic powder
1 teaspoon onion powder
½ teaspoon sea salt
¼ teaspoon freshly ground black pepper
¼ teaspoon paprika
½ cup toasted sesame seeds
1 egg, slightly beaten
1 teaspoon water
1 pound white meat chicken, cut into 1-inch strips
2 tablespoons coconut oil or Ghee (page 234)

1. Combine the first 7 ingredients on a flat dinner plate.
2. Combine the egg and water in a shallow bowl.
3. Dip the chicken into the egg mixture and then into the sesame seed mixture. Place the coated chicken on a flat plate (see Cook's Note below).
4. Heat the oil in a large frying pan over medium heat for 2 minutes, or until hot.
5. Place the coated chicken in the hot oil, being careful not to overcrowd the pan, and cook for about 3 minutes per side, or until nicely browned.
6. Continue until all the chicken is cooked. Add more oil if needed, and lower the heat if the pan starts to get too hot.
7. Serve immediately with Peach and Pineapple Dipping Sauce (page 267), or with any of the sauces found in the Sauces and Condiments section of this book (page 247).

Cook's Note: You can prepare these tenders in advance and, when you reach the indicated step, store the raw, coated tenders in the refrigerator until you are ready to cook them. They only take 6 minutes to cook, so this is a very quick main dish.

Lamb with Apricots and Prunes Tagine

The word "tagine" refers to either a stew, or a Moroccan cooking vessel. This is a flavorful stew with exotic spices, lamb and dried fruits that can be cooked in a tagine or in the oven.

Prep time: 25 minutes

Cook time: 1½-2 hours, or until meat is tender

Makes: 4 servings

3 tablespoons extra virgin olive oil

1 large onion, sliced

4 cloves garlic, chopped

3-3½ pounds boneless leg of lamb, cut into 2-inch pieces

½ teaspoon sea salt

¼ teaspoon pepper

1 teaspoon dry mustard

½ teaspoon chopped ginger

1 teaspoon turmeric

1 teaspoon garam masala or curry powder

1 cinnamon stick or ¼ teaspoon ground cinnamon

¼ teaspoon cumin

3½ cups Vegetable Stock (page 235) or Chicken Stock (page 240)

1 cup whole dried apricots

1 cup dried prunes, or other mixed dried fruits (without added sugar)

¼ cup sliced almonds (optional)

1. Preheat the oven to 350°F.

2. Heat 2 tablespoons of the oil in a medium-sized frying pan over medium-high heat for 3 minutes, or until hot.

3. Sauté the onion for 5 minutes, or until it begins to brown.

4. Add the garlic and sauté for 2 minutes.

5. Remove the onion and garlic to a 3-quart oven-proof casserole dish with a cover, or to a Dutch oven.

6. Add the remaining oil to the frying pan and heat for 1 minute.

7. Add half of the lamb to the frying pan and brown on all sides for about 5 minutes. Remove the cooked lamb to the casserole dish.

8. Adding more oil as needed, brown the remainder of the lamb in the frying pan. Once cooked, add it to the casserole dish.

9. Combine the salt, pepper and spices and add them, along with the vegetable or chicken stock and the dried fruits, to the casserole dish. Stir well to combine.

10. Cover the casserole dish and cook in the preheated oven for 1½-2 hours, or until the meat is tender.

11. Top with the sliced almonds before serving if desired.

PHASE 3 **variation:** Once you reach Phase 3, you may substitute beef broth, which results in a darker colored, fuller flavored sauce.

Cook's Note: If you prefer, you can cook this recipe in a slow cooker set to Cook on Low for 4-6 hours, or in a tagine on the stovetop for about 1½ hours, or until the meat is tender.

Cran-Raspberry Glazed Salmon

Salmon, which is high in omega-3 fatty acids, is recommended for everyone to eat at least once a week. Here is another enjoyable recipe to help you meet that goal.

Prep time: 10 minutes

Cook time: 8 minutes

Makes: 2 servings

Salmon
¾ pound salmon filet, 1-inch thick
Salt and pepper

Glaze
1 clove garlic, crushed
¼ cup Cran-Raspberry Sauce (page 256)
1 teaspoon mustard
1 teaspoon oat flour
¼ teaspoon sea salt

1. Preheat the oven to Broil.
2. Season the salmon with the salt and pepper and place it on a baking sheet, flesh side up.
3. Combine the glaze ingredients and brush over the flesh side of the salmon.
4. Broil or grill for 8 minutes, or until the fish flakes easily with a fork. Do not turn the salmon while cooking.
5. Serve immediately.

Cook's Note: This glazed salmon is even more delicious when served over greens with mango dressing, to make an entrée salad. Top a cup of baby mixed greens with the cooked, glazed salmon, and dress with two tablespoons of Mango Dressing (page 254).

Roast Rack of Lamb with Mustard Herb Crust

This elegant dinner is ideal for a special occasion. The recipe can easily be doubled, so make this the next time you have company for dinner.

Prep time: 25 minutes

Cook time: 18-30 minutes, depending on desired doneness

Makes: 2 servings

1 teaspoon dry mustard

2 teaspoons raw apple cider vinegar

2 teaspoons chopped chives

2 teaspoons chopped rosemary

1 teaspoon chopped thyme

8 roasted almonds, finely chopped

2 cloves garlic, crushed

¼ teaspoon sea salt

⅛ teaspoon freshly ground black pepper

1 teaspoon honey

1 rack of lamb (6-9 chops), trimmed of most of the fat

1. Preheat the oven to 425ºF.

2. Combine all the ingredients, except for the honey and the lamb, in a small bowl.

3. Using a pastry brush, coat the fat side of the lamb with the honey.

4. Spoon the mustard herb mixture onto the lamb and spread it over the top, pressing it in with your fingers to form a crust.

5. Place the lamb, herb-coated side up, into a heavy frying pan or small roasting pan. Cook in the preheated oven to desired doneness: 18-20 minutes for rare meat, 25 minutes for medium-rare and 30 minutes for medium-well.

6. Cut the rack into chops and serve immediately.

Cook's Note: You can prepare the meat in advance of cooking – season and coat it earlier in the day, so that you can spend time with your guests instead of in the kitchen.

Grilled Chicken Souvlaki

These chicken skewers can be grilled outdoors or in the kitchen. For extra flavor, let them marinate for several hours in the refrigerator.

Prep time: 20 minutes
Cook time: 18-20 minutes

Makes: 4 servings

Marinade
2 tablespoons raw apple cider vinegar
2 tablespoons extra virgin olive oil
¼ teaspoon each sea salt and freshly ground black pepper
1 clove garlic, crushed
¼ teaspoon dry mustard
~~½ teaspoon paprika~~
½ teaspoon dried oregano
½ teaspoon dried thyme
½ teaspoon dried parsley
½ teaspoon dried mint

Chicken
1 pound boneless chicken breasts, cut into 1-inch cubes
8 skewers

Creamy Herb Vinaigrette Sauce
¼ cup Homemade Mayonnaise (page 248)
1 tablespoon Fresh Herb Vinaigrette (page 79)

1. If you are using bamboo skewers, soak them in water for at least 30 minutes.

2. Combine all the marinade ingredients in a plastic freezer bag. Add the chicken cubes and place the bag in the refrigerator to marinate for 30 minutes to 3 hours.

3. Thread the marinated chicken onto the skewers. Grill on an outdoor grill* or on a preheated indoor grill pan for 9-10 minutes per side, or until nicely browned. Turn the skewers once during cooking.

4. Combine the mayonnaise and the herb vinaigrette and serve as a sauce with the grilled, skewered chicken.

Some controversy exists regarding outdoor grilling, because of carcinogens found in grill smoke and in meats cooked over a high heat. To avoid any possible problems, try indirect grilling, as explained in the Cook's Note below.

Cook's Note: Start the fire to one side of the grill, rather than in the center. Then, when the fire and the grill grates are hot, cook next to the fire rather than directly over it, with the grill cover down. This method, called indirect grilling, can be used for cooking large cuts of meat and whole turkeys, as well as for smaller items like these chicken skewers.

Coconut Chicken Tenders

Kids and adults love chicken tenders, so try this healthy, easy-to-make version. Serve them with Corn Fritters (page 170) and Peach and Pineapple Dipping Sauce (page 267).

Prep time: 20 minutes
Cook time: 10 minutes

Makes: 4 servings

1 egg

2 tablespoons coconut kefir or Coconut Milk (page 237)

½ cup unsweetened coconut

½ cup Almond Meal (page 236)

½ teaspoon sea salt

½ teaspoon garlic powder

¼ teaspoon paprika

12 ounces skinless, white meat chicken strips

2 tablespoons coconut oil

1. Combine the egg and the kefir or milk in a shallow dish.

2. Combine the remaining ingredients, except for the chicken and the oil or ghee, on a flat plate.

3. Dip the chicken into the egg mixture.

4. Dredge the egged chicken in the coconut mixture.

5. Heat 1 tablespoon of the oil or ghee in a medium-sized frying pan over medium-high heat for about 2 minutes, or until hot.

6. Add half the tenders to the hot oil, being careful not to overcrowd the pan, and cook for 3-5 minutes per side, or until golden brown.

7. Add the remaining oil if needed, and cook the rest of the tenders.

Nutrition Note: Of all the foods in nature, coconuts contain the highest level (50%) of lauric acid, which is a powerful tool to enhance the immune system. Clinical studies have shown that lauric acid has anti-microbial and anti-viral properties.

Mixed Herb Pesto with Brown Rice Pasta

This recipe is a twist on standard pesto, which is typically made with just basil leaves and pine nuts. The inclusion of parsley, chives and almonds adds a new dimension to this easy sauce.

Prep time: 15 minutes
Cook time: 12 minutes

. . . .

Makes: 2 servings
(½ cup pesto)

. . . .

4 ounces brown rice pasta

1 cup packed basil leaves

2 tablespoons roughly chopped chives

¼ cup parsley leaves, stems removed

1 tablespoon pine nuts

1 tablespoon sliced almonds

1 small clove garlic

¼ teaspoon sea salt

¼ cup extra virgin olive oil

1. Cook the pasta according to the package directions.

2. While the pasta is cooking, place all the remaining ingredients, except for the oil, into a food processor and pulse until the herbs are completely chopped.

3. Drizzle the oil down the feed tube and continue to process until all the oil is incorporated.

4. Reserve a tablespoon or two of the pasta water before draining the pasta.

5. Toss the drained pasta with the pesto. If necessary, add some of the reserved pasta water to thin the pesto. Serve immediately.

. . . .

PHASE 3 **Variation:** Once you reach Phase 3, you can stir 2 tablespoons of grated Parmesan cheese into the pesto before tossing it with the pasta. Top the pasta with chopped plum tomatoes and additional grated cheese.

. . . .

Cook's Note: Not in the mood for pasta? Try this pesto as a topping for broiled chicken or fish, or add some to Homemade Mayonnaise (page 248) for a tasty salad dressing.

Pavlova

This recipe was named after the famous Russian ballerina, Anna Pavlova. In this version, a base of meringue shell is topped with Zabaglione Sauce and fresh berries.

Prep time: 15 minutes

Cook time: 2 hours

Set up time: 24 hours

....

Makes: 4 meringue shells

....

2 egg whites

¼ cup xylitol

½ teaspoon raw apple
cider vinegar

1 teaspoon vanilla

¾ cup Zabaglione Sauce
(page 251)

Assorted mixed berries

1. Preheat the oven to 225°F.
2. Using an electric mixer, beat the egg whites on Medium speed for about 30 seconds, or until blended.
3. Place the xylitol in a food processor and process until it is reduced to a fine powder.
4. Raise the speed of the mixer to High and add the vinegar.
5. Add the xylitol to the egg whites 1 tablespoon at a time while still mixing on High for about 1½ minutes, until stiff glossy peaks form.
6. Add the vanilla and mix for about 20 seconds.
7. Line a baking sheet with parchment paper.
8. Measure out 4 portions of meringue using a ½-cup measuring cup, and drop each onto the parchment-lined baking sheet, leaving a few inches of space between each shell.
9. Using a spoon or spatula, make a well in the center of each shell, so that it looks like a nest.
10. Bake in the preheated oven for 2 hours. Remove the meringues from the oven, but take care not to touch them, as they will be sticky.
11. Allow the shells to stand uncovered and set up for 12 hours, or until fully hardened, before removing them from the tray.
12. Fill the shells with the Zabaglione Sauce, top with the berries and serve.

Cook's Note: Unused shells will keep for weeks in a cookie tin, if stored in a cool, dry place.

Honey Nut Bars

These delicious bars are perfect for a snack or for dessert. You may substitute any allowable nuts for those given in the recipe. Remember that sweets should be kept to a minimum, so make these a special treat.

Prep time: 15 minutes

Cook time: 15 minutes

Makes: 9 bars

¼ cup Ghee (page 234) or margarine, heated

½ cup honey

½ teaspoon cinnamon

½ cup Almond Meal (page 236) or Almond Flour (page 236)

2 tablespoons brown rice flour

½ cup cashews

½ cup pecan halves

½ cup almonds

½ cup walnuts

1. Preheat the oven to 350ºF.

2. Combine the ghee or margarine, honey and cinnamon in a small bowl.

3. Combine the remaining ingredients, and stir in the honey mixture.

4. Grease an 8x8x2-inch pan, and line the pan with parchment paper, trimming the edges.

5. Spoon the mixture into the prepared pan. Press the mixture down until the bottom of the pan is evenly covered.

6. Bake in the preheated oven for 15 minutes, or until the edges just start to brown.

7. Remove the pan from the oven and allow to cool for about 30 minutes.

8. Place the pan in the refrigerator for several hours to harden.

9. Once the mixture has hardened, cut it into bars. To store, wrap each bar in plastic wrap and keep refrigerated for up to 3 weeks.

Cook's Note: The bars are very sticky and will be difficult to remove from the pan if parchment paper is not used, or if the bars have not sufficiently hardened. Do not use waxed paper, because the bars will stick to it.

Pumpkin Custard

This recipe brings Thanksgiving to mind because it tastes like pumpkin pie without the crust.

Prep time: 15 minutes

Cook time: 1 hour 20 minutes
....

Makes: 5 servings
....

2 eggs

1 cup Almond Milk (page 237)

3 tablespoons agave nectar

2 tablespoons maple syrup

1 cup canned or cooked pumpkin

½ teaspoon vanilla

¼ teaspoon sea salt

1 teaspoon cinnamon

½ teaspoon freshly grated ginger

¼ teaspoon allspice

⅛ teaspoon nutmeg

1. Preheat the oven to 350°F.

2. Combine all the ingredients in a large bowl. Mix well using a wire whisk or hand mixer.

3. Pour ½ cup of the mixture into each of 5 custard cups.

4. Place the cups in a 13x9-inch baking dish. Fill the baking dish with enough hot water to reach about ⅓ of the way up the sides of the cups, being careful not to get any water into the cups.

5. Bake in the preheated oven for 1 hour and 10-20 minutes, or until the custards are set, their tops are shiny, and a knife inserted about 2 inches from a cup's center comes out clean.

6. Carefully remove the custards from the water bath and allow them to cool for 30 minutes, or refrigerate and serve chilled.

Nutrition Note: As a rule of thumb, the deeper the color of a fruit or vegetable, the higher the nutritional content. Pumpkin, being a bright orange, is a rich source of vitamins and minerals, particularly beta-carotene, vitamin C and potassium.

Mint Tea

Mint tea is as refreshing on a cold night as it is a on a hot summer day. If you like mint, give this super simple recipe a try.

Prep time: 15 minutes

Makes: 1 cup

¼ cup mint leaves
1 cup boiling water

1. Place the mint leaves in the boiling water and allow them to steep for up to 10 minutes.

2. Strain the mint leaves from the water, and drink immediately.

PHASE 2 **Variation:** Add a 1-inch slice of peeled ginger to the mint leaves and steep for 10 minutes to make Ginger Mint Tea.

Nutrition Note: Peppermint is said to have an antispasmodic effect on the muscles, so herbalists use it to treat respiratory problems and to soothe stomach cramps, irritable bowel symptoms and nausea. Ginger is also said to have soothing properties for upset stomachs, and its anti-inflammatory properties might help with migraine headaches, muscle aches and joint pain. Combining these two herbs can help to alleviate a variety of ailments. Most importantly, the tea tastes great!

Ice Cookies

Why "Ice Cookies"? Xylitol, the sweetener used in this recipe, is the same one that gives sugarless gum its cool taste. Apparently, this effect works on cookies as well. These cookies are unlike any you have ever had.

Prep time: 15 minutes

Cook time: 2 hours

Set up time: 24 hours

Makes: about 15 cookies, half almond flavor and half coconut flavor

2 egg whites

¼ cup xylitol

½ teaspoon raw apple cider vinegar

1 teaspoon vanilla extract

¼ cup toasted almonds, chopped

¼ cup coconut

1. Preheat the oven to 225°F.
2. Using an electric mixer, beat the egg whites on Medium speed for about 30 seconds, or until blended.
3. Place the xylitol in a food processor and process until it is reduced to a fine powder.
4. Raise the speed of the mixer to High and add the vinegar.
5. Add the xylitol to the egg whites 1 tablespoon at a time while still mixing on High for about 1½ minutes, until stiff glossy peaks form.
6. Add the vanilla and mix for about 20 seconds.
7. Divide the meringue into two equal parts. Fold the toasted nuts into one half and the coconut into the other.
8. Line a baking sheet with waxed or parchment paper. Drop the meringue onto the baking sheet by well-rounded tablespoonfuls.
9. Bake in the preheated oven for 2 hours.
10. Turn the oven off and allow the meringues to cool completely, and to stand for several hours or overnight until they have fully hardened before removing them from the tray.
11. Store the cookies in a covered metal tin.

Cook's Commentary: Originally, this recipe was titled "Meringue Cookies," but when we first tested it, the meringues didn't harden like they were supposed to. We declared the recipe a failure, and abandoned the cookies on the counter overnight. By the next morning, a strange thing had happened: the cookies had finally hardened and looked the way meringues should, but when we tried them, they tasted cold. We loved them!

Blueberry Coconut Ice Cream

This ice cream is creamy, delectable and – amazingly – 100% dairy-free! You will need an electric ice cream maker to make this recipe. If you have never made ice cream before, don't be afraid to try. The steps are simple, and the ice cream maker does most of the work.

Prep time: 15 minutes
Cook time: 5 minutes
Cool time: 30 minutes
Freeze time: 30 minutes

....

Makes: 1 pint
(4 standard scoops)

....

½ cup Coconut Milk (page 237)

Pinch of sea salt

1 egg yolk

½ teaspoon vanilla extract

2 cups blueberries

2 tablespoons water

3 tablespoons raw honey

1. Heat the coconut milk and salt in a small saucepan over medium-high heat for 3 minutes, or until it reaches a boil. Reduce the heat to medium-low.

2. Place the egg yolk in a small bowl. Remove 2 tablespoons of boiled coconut milk from the saucepan (do not remove the pan from the heat), and very slowly whisk it into the egg yolk.

3. When the milk and egg yolk are incorporated, whisk the mixture into the heated coconut milk and cook, stirring constantly with a wooden spoon, until the mixture thickens to a custard-like consistency that coats the back of the spoon (this should take 3-5 minutes). Constant stirring is needed to ensure the yolk does not curdle.

4. As soon as the mixture thickens, remove the pan from the heat, immediately pour it into a small bowl to cool and stir in the vanilla.

5. Place the mixture in the refrigerator to cool for about 30 minutes.

6. Meanwhile, place the blueberries, water and honey in the bowl of a food processor. Pulse about 10 times until the berries are chopped, but not liquefied.

7. Combine the blueberries and custard mixture in the bowl of an electric ice cream maker. Follow the instructions that came with your ice cream maker to freeze the ice cream.

8. If the ice cream is not quite hard enough to scoop immediately, place it in the freezer for 30 minutes to firm it up.

Cook's Note: If you are storing leftover ice cream in your freezer, you might need to allow it to soften for a few minutes before serving. Some freezers are colder than others, so use your judgment.

Iced Minted Raspberry Green Tea

Cool and refreshing on a summer day or anytime, this tea is a perfect substitute for soft drinks and other calorie-laden drinks. Your whole family will love this recipe!

Prep time: 5 minutes

Cool time: 2 hours

Makes: about 6 cups

4 cups water

¼-½ cup xylitol

1 cup fresh or frozen raspberries

4 green tea bags

2 cups ice cubes

2 sprigs fresh mint

6 sprigs fresh mint (garnish)

1. Combine the water, xylitol and raspberries in a 2-quart saucepot and stir well to distribute the xylitol. Bring the mixture to a boil, and boil for about 5 minutes to make a simple syrup. Reduce the heat to medium and simmer for 5 minutes.

2. Position a sieve in a bowl. Pour the mixture through the sieve and mash the raspberries with a spoon to squeeze out the juice while leaving the seeds in the sieve.

3. Immerse the tea bags in the liquid and allow the tea to steep for 4 minutes.

4. Allow the tea to cool, and then pour it into a pitcher, add the mint and refrigerate until ready to serve.

5. Add the ice to the pitcher just before serving. Serve in tall, ice-filled glasses, and garnish with the mint sprigs.

Cook's Note: If you prefer to use honey to sweeten the tea, eliminate the xylitol and continue as directed above. After the tea has cooled to 115°F, stir in ¼ cup raw honey, and then serve as directed.

Nutrition Note: Green tea contains antioxidants called "catechins" that help destroy free radicals, which contribute to cancer and blood clots and can damage DNA. Raspberries are also high in antioxidants, and mint is rich in vitamins A, C and B12, thiamine, folic acid and riboflavin, as well as in essential minerals, including manganese, copper, potassium, iron, calcium, zinc, phosphorus, fluoride and selenium.

Applesauce Walnut Tea Bread, page 158

Phase 3
Contents

Phase 3: The Late Reentry Phase *(four weeks)*

Phase 3 of the Lyme Inflammation Diet® is to be followed for four weeks after the conclusion of Phase 2. Do not begin Phase 3 until you are certain the foods you reintroduced in Phase 2 have not triggered new bouts of inflammatory symptoms. If symptoms do recur, wait until they subside before moving on to the next Phase.

During Phase 3, your goal is to reintroduce additional foods that are normally healthy, but can trigger inflammation in some people. All these foods have a greater risk of doing so than the foods listed in Phase 2, so proceed cautiously, once again reintroducing Phase 3 foods no sooner than one every other day. Should health problems occur as a result of eating these additional foods, return to Phase 2 until you feel better. (The food and beverages that pose the highest risk of triggering inflammation during Phase 3 are indicated with an asterisk.)

At this point, you may include soybeans in your diet, but avoid soy milk, textured soy protein meat substitutes and soy powders. Instead, choose fermented soy foods, such as miso, natto and tempeh. Tofu is permissible as well, but fermented soy foods are better choices.

As a food group, grains carry a higher than normal risk of causing inflammation, particularly those with the highest gluten content (wheat, barley, rye). Therefore, proceed with caution as you reintroduce grains to your diet. Whole grain pasta made from Phase 3 allowable grains is also acceptable, provided no adverse reactions occur.

Proceed with caution when reintroducing nightshade foods (chilies, eggplant, peppers (both red and green), white potatoes and tomatoes, as well as the spices cayenne, chili powder and paprika), which can cause inflammation. You might need to avoid these foods altogether if you know you are sensitive to them, or if you suffer from arthritis symptoms that are aggravated by them.

Dairy is another food group with a higher than normal risk of causing inflammation. Proceed with caution as you reintroduce dairy products, and avoid them altogether if you are allergic or sensitive to them.

Foods Allowed During Phase 3

Beverages
Apple juice [5]
Citrus juice*
Coffee (organic)*
Orange juice [5]

Fruits
Apple (all varieties)
Banana [5]
Grapefruit*
Lemon*
Lime*
Nectarine
Orange*
Peach
Strawberry*

Nuts/Seeds
Peanuts*[1]
Pistachios*[1] NEW

Vegetables
Dill pickles NEW
Jicama NEW

Nightshade Foods
Cayenne*
Chili powder*
Chilies*
Eggplant*
Green pepper*
Hot pepper*
Mild pepper*
Paprika*
Potato (white)*
Red pepper*
Tomato*

Grains
Barley *
Buckwheat
Corn*
Groats
Millet
Oats
Quinoa
Rye
Sorghum NEW
Sprouted grain breads
Teff NEW
Wheat* (including)
  Durum*[2]
  Einkorn*[2]
  Faro*[2]
  Kamut*[2]
  Semolina*[2]
  Spelt*[2]

Traditional Soy Bean Products
Miso
Natto NEW
Tamari
Tempah
Tofu

Protein Sources
Beef
Bison (free-range)
Chicken (dark meat)
Turkey (dark meat)

Dairy
Butter (organic)
Cheeses*[3]
Milk*[3]
Cream*[3]
Yogurt *[3,4]

Fats
Almond oil NEW
Avocado oil NEW
Grapeseed oil NEW
Palm oil NEW
Safflower oil NEW
Sunflower seed oil NEW

Other
Air-popped popcorn NEW
Arrowroot NEW
Baking powder NEW
Guar gum NEW
Other vinegars NEW
Xanthan gum NEW

---

* These foods and beverages pose the highest risk of triggering inflammation.

[1] Have a high risk of mold, so buy raw and organic, and store in the refrigerator.

[2] From the wheat family, so use very cautiously.

[3] Raw cow or goat milk sources are highly preferable.

[4] Plain, unsweetened and organic (if possible).

[5] Use sparingly, as they are very high in sugar.

Toasted Coconut Almond Muffins

The combination of toasted coconut and almonds gives these gluten-free muffins a nutty flavor and delightful chewy texture.

Prep time: 20 minutes

Cook time: 15-20 minutes

Makes: 6 muffins

½ cup unsweetened coconut

¾ cup Gluten-Free Baking Mix (page 241)

2 tablespoons Almond Meal (page 236)

1 tablespoon brown rice flour

1 tablespoon tapioca flour

½ teaspoon xanthan gum

2 tablespoons honey

¼ cup maple syrup

1 egg

⅓ cup safflower oil or Ghee (page 234)

½ cup Almond Milk (page 237)

½ teaspoon almond extract

1. Preheat the oven to 350ºF.

2. Grease a 6-cup muffin pan and set aside.

3. Place the coconut on a small baking dish and toast in the preheated oven for 5 minutes, or until golden brown. Watch carefully, because coconut can burn very quickly. Allow to cool slightly.

4. Combine the gluten-free mix, almond meal, flours, xanthan gum and the cooled, toasted coconut in a medium-sized bowl.

5. Combine the wet ingredients, add them to the dry ingredients and stir.

6. Fill each muffin cup with a scant ⅓ cup of batter.

7. Bake in the preheated oven for 20-25 minutes, or until a toothpick inserted in the center of a muffin comes out clean.

Applesauce Walnut Tea Bread

Apples and cinnamon always pair well. Cinnamon Applesauce and chopped apples give this bread intense apple flavor.

Prep time: 20 minutes

Cook time: 45 minutes

. . . .

Makes: 1 loaf

. . . .

2 cups Gluten-Free Baking Mix (page 241)

½ cup xylitol

2 eggs

½ cup Cinnamon Applesauce (page 250)

¼ cup Almond Milk (page 237)

1 teaspoon cinnamon

¼ teaspoon ginger

1 teaspoon vanilla

½ cup safflower oil

½ cup chopped walnuts

1 green apple, peeled and chopped

1. Preheat the oven to 350ºF.
2. Combine the baking mix and xylitol in a mixing bowl and set aside.
3. Combine the remaining ingredients, except for the walnuts and the apple.
4. Using a rubber spatula, stir the wet ingredients into the dry ingredients until just combined.
5. Stir in the walnuts and apple.
6. Grease an 8x8x2-inch loaf pan. Spoon the batter into the loaf pan.
7. Bake in the preheated oven for 45 minutes, or until the top is nicely browned and a toothpick inserted in the center comes out clean.

Cook's Note: The batter for this recipe can be made into 6 muffins, rather than a loaf. To make muffins, preheat the oven to 400ºF and bake for 20 minutes, or until a toothpick inserted in the center of a muffin comes out clean.

Gluten-Free Blueberry Lemon Muffins

Lemon zest and juice add extra flavor to these gluten-free blueberry muffins.

Prep time: 15 minutes

Cook time: 20 minutes

Makes: 6 muffins

1⅓ cups Gluten-Free Baking Mix (page 241)

⅓ cup xylitol

1 egg

4 tablespoons Ghee (page 234) or melted margarine

½ cup Almond Milk (page 237)

Zest of 1 lemon

1 teaspoon lemon juice

1 teaspoon vanilla

¾ cups fresh or frozen blueberries

1. Preheat the oven to 400°F.
2. Combine the baking mix and xylitol in a mixing bowl and set aside.
3. Combine the remaining ingredients, except for the blueberries.
4. Using a rubber spatula or wooden spoon, stir the wet ingredients into the dry ingredients until just combined.
5. Stir in the blueberries.
6. Grease a 6-cup muffin pan. Using a ⅓-cup measuring cup, fill each of the muffin cups with batter.
7. Bake in the preheated oven for 20 minutes, or until the tops are nicely browned and a toothpick inserted in the center of a muffin comes out clean.

Cook's Note: Try different flavor combinations using your favorite citrus and fruit. For example, substitute orange for lemon and fruit-juice sweetened, dried cranberries for blueberries.

Mango Pineapple Smoothie

Kefir has a similar flavor to plain yogurt, and is a pleasant way to get some probiotics while you are taking antibiotics. Drink this smoothie for dessert or breakfast, or even take it to work for lunch.

Prep time: 5 minutes

Makes: 2 cups

½ cup cows' milk kefir

1 tablespoon orange juice

1 cup chopped mango (½ mango)

½ cup chopped fresh pineapple

2 teaspoons raw honey

½ teaspoon vanilla

½ cup ice cubes

1. Place all the ingredients in a blender container. Cover, and blend on High, or on a frozen drink setting, until smooth.

Cook's Note: Use this recipe as a template, and substitute fruits or berries that are in season, or that you especially like.

Millet and Cornmeal Pancakes

These gluten-free pancakes are delicious with maple syrup, or topped with peaches and berries.

Prep time: 15 minutes

Cook time: 10-15 minutes

. . . .

Makes: 10 pancakes

. . . .

1 cup **Millet Flour** (page 242)

½ cup **cornmeal**

2 teaspoons **baking powder**

¼ teaspoon **sea salt**

1 teaspoon **cinnamon**

2 **eggs, separated**

1 tablespoon **Ghee (page 234) or safflower oil**

¾ cup **Almond Milk or Coconut Milk (page 237)**

2 tablespoons **Cinnamon Applesauce (page 250)**

1. Combine the dry ingredients.

2. Beat the egg whites until they form soft peaks. Set them aside.

3. Combine the egg yolks with the remaining ingredients, and stir the mixture into the dry ingredients.

4. Preheat a frying pan or griddle over medium heat for about 5 minutes, or until water sprinkled on the surface sizzles.

5. Fold the beaten egg whites into the batter.

6. Using a ⅓-cup measuring cup, pour enough batter for 1 pancake onto the hot griddle and cook for 1½-2 minutes per side, or until golden brown. Repeat until all the pancakes are cooked.

7. Serve with your favorite toppings.

Cook's Note: Cornmeal can be ground either finely or coarsely (coarse cornmeal is commonly used for grits). You can use either type for this recipe. Coarser cornmeal will give a more gritty texture to the pancakes.

Broccoli, Red Cabbage and Quinoa

This extremely nutritious side dish is as beautiful as it is tasty.

Prep time: 25 minutes
(including soak time)

Cook time: 20 minutes

....

Makes: 4 servings

....

1 cup quinoa

1½ cups Vegetable Stock
(page 240)

4 ounces broccoli florets

4 ounces red cabbage, cut
into 1-inch pieces

¼ cup Ghee (page 234) or
melted margarine

1 teaspoon raw apple cider
vinegar

½ teaspoon dry mustard

½ teaspoon each garlic
powder and onion
powder

½ teaspoon sea salt

¼ teaspoon freshly ground
black pepper

1. Soak the quinoa in a large bowl of water for 15 minutes, or, if using presoaked quinoa, proceed directly to Step 2.

2. Bring the vegetable stock to a boil in a small saucepot over medium heat.

3. While the stock is coming to a boil, rinse the quinoa in a small mesh strainer for 3 minutes.

4. Add the quinoa to the stock and cook for about 18-20 minutes, or until the quinoa resembles small beads and the broth has evaporated.

5. While the quinoa cooks, steam the broccoli and red cabbage together for about 6 minutes, or until tender.

6. While the broccoli and cabbage steam, combine the ghee or margarine, vinegar, mustard, garlic and onion powders and salt and pepper in a small frying pan and heat for 1 minute.

7. Combine the vegetables and the quinoa in a serving bowl.

8. Pour the ghee mixture over the vegetables and quinoa and toss well to coat.

Nutrition Note: The World Health Organization has rated the quality of protein in quinoa as at least equivalent to that in milk. Quinoa offers more iron than other grains and contains high levels of potassium and riboflavin, as well as vitamin B6, niacin and thiamin. It is also a good source of magnesium, zinc, copper and manganese, and has some folic acid.

Bok Choy and Tomato Stir Fry

You don't often see tomatoes in Chinese recipes, but in this recipe, they provide a sweetness that contrasts nicely with the saltiness of the tamari.

Prep time: 5 minutes
Cook time: 5 minutes

Makes: 4 servings

2 tablespoons grapeseed oil

3 scallions, white part only, sliced

2 cloves garlic, crushed

1 small head of bok choy, sliced into 1-inch pieces on the diagonal

1½ tablespoons tamari

1 cup chopped fresh ripe tomato

½ teaspoon sea salt

¼ teaspoon freshly ground black pepper

1. Heat 1 tablespoon of the oil in a large frying pan or wok for 2 minutes, or until hot.
2. Stir fry the scallions in the oil for 30 seconds.
3. Add the garlic and stir fry for 30 seconds.
4. Add the bok choy and tamari and stir fry for 1 minute, or until the bok choy starts to wilt.
5. Stir in the tomato, salt and pepper and stir fry for 2 minutes.

Cook's Note: Chinese cabbage and napa cabbage are two names for the same vegetable. They are sometimes mistaken for a third vegetable, bok choy. The most visible difference between napa cabbage and bok choy is that napa is a lighter green color than the darker green bok choy. Napa cabbage looks a bit like romaine lettuce, but with a curly, Swiss chard-like leaf. It has a mild flavor with a peppery kick that's wonderful in salads or stir fries. Bok choy looks more like Swiss chard, but with pale green stalks and dark green leaves. It has a mild, cabbage-like flavor. Either vegetable works well in this recipe, so use whichever is available at the market.

Soft Pita Wraps

Use these gluten-free pita wraps for sandwiches, or with Greek Ground Lamb Crumble (page 184).

Prep time: 10 minutes
Cook time: 10 minutes

Makes: 4 (9-inch) pita wraps

¾ cup brown rice **flour**
½ cup potato flour
2 tablespoons tapioca flour
1½ teaspoons xanthan gum
½ teaspoon sea salt
½ teaspoon honey
1 cup warm water
Grapeseed or safflower oil

1. Place all the ingredients, except for the oil, in a medium-sized bowl. Stir to combine until the mixture forms a very soft dough.

2. Divide the dough into 4 equal-sized pieces.

3. Generously flour a board with some brown rice flour.

4. Place one of the dough balls on the board, flour the top-side of the dough ball and cover it with a piece of plastic or waxed paper. Using a rolling pin, roll the dough into a 9-inch circle.

5. Roll out the remaining dough balls, and stack the flattened wraps on a plate or tray, separated by plastic wrap so they don't stick together.

6. Heat a large frying pan or griddle (preferably cast iron), or another type of heavy-bottomed pan, over medium-high heat for 5 minutes, or until hot. It should not be too hot, or the wraps will burn.

7. Before making the first pita, wipe the frying pan or griddle with a folded paper towel soaked in 1 teaspoon of oil.

8. Cook each pita for 1 minute per side, or until lightly browned.

9. Stack the cooked pitas on a tray, separated by waxed paper.

Cook's Note: You can store the fully-cooled pita wraps in a plastic bag and refrigerate for later use. They can also be frozen, and then reheated for a few minutes in a 350°F oven or a toaster oven.

Chicken Wild Rice and Vegetable Soup

Chicken soup is the ultimate comfort food. In this version, brown and wild rice add texture. Served with one of the many salads found in this book, this soup is ideal for lunch or a light supper.

Prep time: 20 minutes

Cook time: about 1 hour 20 minutes

. . . .

Makes: about 3½ quarts

. . . .

2 tablespoons extra virgin olive oil

1 onion, cut into 1-inch pieces

3 cloves garlic, chopped

3 carrots, peeled and diced

1 medium zucchini, diced

3 stalks celery, sliced

1 can (28 ounces) diced tomatoes, with liquid

2 quarts Chicken Stock (page 240)

1 cup uncooked brown and wild rice mix

½ teaspoon sea salt

¼ teaspoon freshly ground black pepper

1½ cups cooked chicken, cut into ½-inch pieces

1. Heat the oil in a 4-quart saucepot over medium-high heat for 3 minutes, or until hot.

2. Sauté the onion over medium heat for about 3 minutes, or until limp.

3. Add the garlic, carrots and zucchini and sauté for 5 minutes.

4. Add the remaining ingredients, except for the chicken, and stir well to combine.

5. Bring the soup to a boil over medium-high heat. Lower the heat to medium and simmer for 45 minutes.

6. Add the chicken and cook for 30 minutes.

7. Refrigerate or freeze any leftover soup.

Cook's Note: You can make beef and vegetable soup by substituting beef broth and cooked beef for the chicken, or you can make minestrone by substituting cooked beans for the rice and eliminating the chicken.

Butternut Squash and Apple Soup

Butternut squash and apples are staples of the fall harvest. Here, they combine to make a warm, tasty soup with a spicy, nutty flavor.

Prep time: 30 minutes

Cook time: 50 minutes

....

Makes: 6 servings

....

1 large shallot, minced

1 clove garlic, chopped

1 butternut squash (about 1½ pounds), peeled, seeded and cut into 1-inch pieces

2 tart apples, peeled, seeded and cut into 1-inch pieces

1 teaspoon curry powder

½ teaspoon cumin

¼ teaspoon allspice

¼ teaspoon nutmeg

½ teaspoon freshly chopped rosemary

1 teaspoon sea salt

¼ teaspoon freshly ground black pepper

2 tablespoons extra virgin olive oil

2 tablespoons honey

2½ cups Chicken Stock (page 240)

1 tablespoon Coconut Milk (page 237) or plain yogurt* (optional)

1. Preheat the oven to 425°F.

2. Place the shallot, garlic, squash and apples on a baking sheet that has sides.

3. Combine all the spices and the salt and pepper and sprinkle them over the vegetables in the pan.

4. Pour the oil and honey over the vegetables, toss well to coat and bake in the preheated oven for 40 minutes, or until they start to caramelize.

5. Place the roasted vegetables in a food processor with 1 cup of the chicken stock. Puree until smooth.

6. Pour the pureed mixture into a saucepan and add the remaining stock. Stir well and cook for 10 minutes.

7. Serve hot, with the coconut milk or a dollop of yogurt if desired.

No longer a dairy-free recipe if the optional plain yogurt is added.

Cook's Note: This soup can be made a day in advance and reheated. It also freezes very well, so if you have extra squash and apples to use up, why not make a double batch and freeze it for future use?

Corn Fritters

Corn fresh from the farm is a special treat. There's no need to cook it – just cut it from the cob and add it to your recipes. When corn is out of season, substitute defrosted frozen corn.

Prep time: 10 minutes
Cook time: 6 minutes

Makes: 8 fritters

1½ cups corn, fresh and uncooked, or defrosted frozen

1 egg

½ cup Almond Milk (page 237)

½ cup spelt flour

1 teaspoon baking powder

½ teaspoon each onion powder and garlic powder

¼ teaspoon sea salt

⅛ teaspoon freshly ground black pepper

2-4 tablespoons extra virgin olive oil or Ghee (page 234)

1. Combine all the ingredients, except for the oil, in a mixing bowl.

2. Heat 2 tablespoons of the oil or ghee in a frying pan for 2-3 minutes, or until hot.

3. Ladle about ¼ cup of batter per fritter into the hot oil. Cook the fritter for about 2-3 minutes per side, or until golden brown.

4. Add more oil as needed and continue until all the fritters are cooked.

Cook's Note: Cook only 3-4 fritters at a time, so as not to overcrowd the pan. Place the cooked fritters on a baking tray and keep them warm in a 250°F oven while you make the remaining fritters.

Roasted Vegetables

These colorful vegetables are a great side to serve with Seared Peppered London Broil (page 179).

Prep time: 15 minutes

Cook time: 50 minutes

Makes: 6 servings

1 medium-sized (1 pound) eggplant, unpeeled

1 large (12 ounce) zucchini

1 red, yellow or green pepper, seeded and cut in half lengthwise

1 red onion, peeled

2 carrots peeled, cut into 1-inch pieces

2 dozen whole cherry tomatoes

½ teaspoon sea salt

½ teaspoon freshly ground black pepper

1 teaspoon each garlic powder and onion powder

¼ cup extra virgin olive oil

1. Preheat the oven to 425ºF.

2. Cut all the vegetables, except for the tomatoes, into equal-sized pieces (about 1-inch pieces).

3. Place the vegetables, including the tomatoes, in a single layer on a large baking sheet.

4. Combine the salt, pepper, garlic powder and onion powder and sprinkle the mixture evenly over the vegetables. Toss well to coat.

5. Drizzle the oil evenly over the vegetables and toss again.

6. Place the tray in the preheated oven and cook for 40 minutes. Midway through cooking, carefully remove the tray from the oven and turn the vegetables with a large spoon.

7. After 40 minutes, turn the heat up to 500°F and cook for 10 minutes to caramelize the vegetables, but keep a close eye on them so they don't burn.

Cook's Note: If you prepare these vegetables at the same time as the Seared Peppered London Broil, the steak and the vegetables will be in the oven together for the last 10 minutes of cooking. In that case, the temperature for those 10 minutes should be 550ºF. Read both recipes carefully, so that you can plan your cooking strategy. Alternatively, serve these roasted vegetables over pasta for a beautiful, healthy, vegetarian meal.

Summer Vegetable Medley Salad

Summer is when vegetables are at their freshest and most flavorful, so it's the ideal time of year to serve this steamed and raw salad tossed with a sweet citrus dressing.

Prep time: 20 minutes

Standing time: 1 hour

Makes: 6 servings

1 cup fresh corn kernels

4 ounces snow peas

1 cup julienned green beans

1 cup finely shredded red cabbage

1 cup julienned carrots

Citrus Dressing

⅓ cup extra virgin olive oil

1 lemon, zested and juiced

½ orange, zested and juiced

½ teaspoon each garlic powder and onion powder

2 teaspoons freshly chopped chives

1 teaspoon freshly chopped thyme

1 teaspoon mustard

¼ teaspoon sea salt

⅛ teaspoon freshly ground black pepper

1 tablespoon raw honey

1. Steam the corn, snow peas and green beans together for 5 minutes, or until they are tender but still crisp.

2. Cool the steamed vegetables in a bowl filled with cold water and ice.

3. Drain the cooked vegetables and combine with the remaining raw vegetables in a serving bowl.

4. Combine the dressing ingredients and whisk thoroughly.

5. When you are ready to serve, pour the dressing over the vegetables. Toss well to coat.

Slow Cooked Baked Beans

Slow cooking gives these tangy baked beans a barbecued flavor.

Prep time: 4 hours and 20 minutes (including soaking the beans)

Cook time: 12 hours

. . . .

Makes: about 5 cups

. . . .

½ **pound dried navy beans**

Water

1 tablespoon extra virgin olive oil

1 medium onion, chopped

2 cloves garlic, finely chopped

1 cup Spicy Ketchup (page 271)

½ **cup maple syrup**

1½ **cups water**

1 tablespoon mustard

1 (2-inch) strip of kombu (optional)

½ **teaspoon freshly ground black pepper**

1. Rinse the dried beans and place them in a 3-quart saucepot. Cover them with several inches of water. Bring the water to a boil over medium-high heat and cook uncovered for 4 minutes.

2. Remove from the heat and allow the beans to soak in the covered pot for 4 hours.

3. Drain the beans and place them in the slow cooker.

4. Heat the oil in a small frying pan over medium-high heat for about 2 minutes, or until hot.

5. Sauté the onion for 3 minutes, or until lightly browned.

6. Add the garlic and sauté for 30 seconds.

7. Add the onion and garlic and the remaining ingredients to the slow cooker, and stir well to combine.

8. Cover the cooker and set it to cook on Low for 12 hours, or until the beans are tender.

Nutrition Note: Kombu is a sea vegetable that is frequently used in Asian cuisine. It is high in vitamins A, B2 and C, calcium and iodine. A member of the kelp family, kombu is used when cooking beans because it helps to make them more digestible. It is usually sold in dried, nearly black strips that soften when immersed in water.

Honey Maple Sweet Potato and Apples

Apples and sweet potatoes evoke thoughts of Thanksgiving. Honey and maple syrup help caramelize the apples and potatoes in this family favorite.

Prep time: 10 minutes

Cook time: about 1 hour

. . . .

Makes: 4 servings

. . . .

1 large (about ¾ pound) sweet potato

1 Granny Smith apple

2 tablespoons honey

3 tablespoons maple syrup

½-1 tablespoon margarine

¼ teaspoon cinnamon

1. Preheat the oven to 425ºF.

2. Partially bake the sweet potato for 30-40 minutes, or until a knife inserted in the center easily slides halfway into the potato.

3. Allow the potato to cool slightly and then peel and cut it into 12 slices.

4. Cut the apple into 12 equal-sized wedges.

5. Arrange the potato and apple slices, alternating, in an 8- or 9-inch round casserole dish or pie plate.

6. Combine the honey and syrup and pour evenly over the slices.

7. Dot the tops of the slices with small pieces of the margarine and sprinkle with the cinnamon.

8. Bake in the preheated oven for 20 minutes. Midway through cooking, carefully remove the dish from the oven and baste the slices with the syrupy liquid. This will help them caramelize. Check frequently to ensure the slices do not over-brown.

Cook's Note: Choose a long, narrow sweet potato, so the potato slices will be about the same size as the apple slices.

Baked Acorn Squash with Applesauce and Almonds

For a sweet, healthy treat, dress up this bland squash with applesauce. This side is a perfect accompaniment to roast turkey or chicken.

Prep time: 10 minutes

Cook time: 1 hour

Makes: 4 servings

½ teaspoon extra virgin olive oil

1 acorn squash (1½-2 pounds), cut in half horizontally, with seeds and fiber removed

¼ teaspoon each garlic powder, onion powder and sea salt

⅛ teaspoon freshly ground black pepper

1 cup water

¼ cup Cinnamon Applesauce (page 250)

1-2 tablespoons maple syrup

¼ teaspoon cinnamon

6 roasted almonds, finely chopped

1 teaspoon margarine

1. Preheat the oven to 425°F.

2. Rub the oil into each of the squash halves.

3. Combine the garlic powder, onion powder, salt and pepper, and sprinkle each of the halves with the mixture.

4. Pour the water into a baking dish with a cover.

5. Place the squash in the baking dish, cut side up. Cover the dish, and bake in the preheated oven for 30 minutes.

6. Carefully remove the dish from the oven. Combine the applesauce, syrup and cinnamon and spoon equal amounts into each half, being sure to spoon some of the applesauce along the top rim of each half.

7. Sprinkle the halves with the nuts and dot with the margarine.

8. Return the baking dish to the oven and bake uncovered for 30 minutes.

Cook's Note: It's important to cover the squash for the first 30 minutes of baking, because the resulting steam bathes the squash in hot water vapor, uniformly cooking the dense vegetable. The squash is then baked uncovered for 30 minutes, to allow the tops to brown slightly.

Millet Coated Fish Filets

Unsweetened puffed millet is not just for breakfast anymore! Grind the cereal in a coffee grinder or food processor until it's reduced to a fine, even texture, and use it in place of breadcrumbs as a delicious, crunchy coating for your fish filets.

Prep time: 15 minutes
Cook time: 10-12 minutes

Makes: 4 servings

1 tablespoon honey

2 tablespoons mustard

1 egg, lightly beaten

1 cup ground unsweetened puffed millet

1 teaspoon each garlic powder and onion powder

¼ teaspoon sea salt

¼ teaspoon freshly ground black pepper

1 pound flounder, sole or tilapia fish filets

2-3 tablespoons coconut oil, grapeseed oil or Ghee (page 234)

1. Combine the honey, mustard and egg in a shallow bowl.

2. Combine the ground millet, garlic and onion powder, salt and pepper on a flat plate.

3. Dip the fish filets into the egg mixture and then into the millet mixture. Coat both sides of each filet with the mixture.

4. Place the coated fish on a flat tray until ready to cook.

5. Heat 2 tablespoons of the oil or ghee in a large frying pan over medium-high heat for 3 minutes, or until hot.

6. Cook the fish about 2-3 minutes per side, depending on the thickness of the filets, or until nicely browned. If the pan appears to be getting too hot, lower the temperature slightly, so as not to burn the coating and undercook the fish. If necessary, cook only a few filets at a time so as not to overcrowd the pan. Add additional oil, if needed.

Cook's Note: This millet coating can be used in any recipe that calls for a coating of breadcrumbs, such as crab cakes, chicken, eggplant or zucchini.

Seared Peppered London Broil

Prep time: 10 minutes

Cook time: 18-24 minutes

Makes: 6 servings

1½-2 teaspoons whole black peppercorns

¼ teaspoon garlic salt

¼ teaspoon onion powder

½ teaspoon sea salt

½ teaspoon Herbes de Provence

1 teaspoon mustard

½ teaspoon honey

2 pounds top round, cut for London broil, cut 1-inch thick

1 teaspoon grapeseed oil

1. Preheat the oven to 500°F.

2. Place the peppercorns on a small tray lined with plastic wrap. Cover the peppercorns with a second piece of plastic wrap. Crack the peppercorns with a meat mallet or rolling pin. Remove the top layer of plastic wrap.

3. Combine the pepper, garlic salt, onion powder, salt and herbs on a flat plate.

4. Combine the mustard and honey.

5. Paint the top of the steak with half the honey mustard.

6. Place the painted side of the steak on the peppercorn mixture and paint the other side of the steak with the remaining honey mustard.

7. Turn the steak over to coat the second side with the peppercorn mixture. The steak should be sparsely coated on both sides with the mixture.

8. Heat a cast iron or heavy-bottomed frying pan over medium-high heat for 8 minutes, or until very hot.

9. Add the oil and tilt the pan so that the oil coats the bottom of the pan.

10. Place the steak in the pan. Cook for 5 minutes to sear one side; then, turn the meat and cook for 5 minutes on the other side.

11. Place the pan in the preheated oven for 10 minutes.*

12. Allow the steak to stand for 5 minutes before slicing. Slice in thin slices on the diagonal, against the grain.

> *The cook time given is for medium-rare meat. If you prefer rare meat, reduce the cook time to 8 minutes. If you prefer well-done meat, cook for 12-14 minutes.*

Cook's Note: Serve with Roasted Vegetables (page 171) if desired.

Multicolored Stuffed Peppers

These stuffed peppers are rich in color and flavor. Use any color of peppers you like, or try the colorful quartet shown in the picture.

Prep time: 30 minutes

Cook time: 45 minutes

. . . .

Makes: 4 servings

. . . .

2 tablespoons grapeseed or safflower oil

1 medium onion, chopped

3 cloves garlic, crushed

1 pound sweet Italian turkey sausage, removed from the casing

¼ cup tomato paste

1 tablespoon freshly chopped parsley

½ teaspoon each freshly chopped thyme and oregano

½ teaspoon sea salt

¼ teaspoon freshly ground pepper

1½ cups fresh or frozen corn kernels

4 whole peppers, tops and seeds removed

2½ cups tomato sauce

1. Preheat the oven to 400ºF.

2. Heat the oil in a large frying pan over medium-high heat for about 2 minutes, or until hot.

3. Sauté the onion for about 3 minutes, or until it starts to brown.

4. Add the garlic and sauté for 30 seconds.

5. Add the sausage meat and cook for about 5 minutes, or until it loses its color.

6. Add the tomato paste and cook for 5 minutes.

7. Add the herbs, salt, pepper and corn, and stir well to combine.

8. Stuff each pepper with the filling mixture, and place in a 13x9x2-inch baking dish.

9. Pour half the tomato sauce into the pan around the peppers. Reserve the rest for later use.

10. Bake in the preheated oven for 45 minutes. Twice during cooking, baste the peppers with the sauce in the pan.

11. Baste the peppers with the remaining sauce, pour the rest of the sauce into the baking dish and serve.

Cook's Note: Easy Oven-Roasted Marinara Sauce (page 258) is perfect for this recipe, and you can save time by making it while you are prepping the pepper stuffing.

Sloppy Joes

This easy to make, Mexican-inspired recipe will be a family favorite. You can make it the night before and reheat to serve – in fact, it tastes even better the second day.

Prep time: 15 minutes
Cook time: 20 minutes

Makes: 4 servings

2 teaspoons extra virgin olive oil

1 small onion, chopped

1 pound ground beef

1 tablespoon chili powder

1 teaspoon garlic powder

1 teaspoon paprika

½ teaspoon cumin

¼ teaspoon sea salt

⅛ teaspoon freshly ground black pepper

1 can (6 ounces) tomato paste

1 cup water

1. Heat the oil in a medium-sized frying pan over medium-high heat for 2 minutes.

2. Add the onion and sauté for about 2 minutes, or until limp.

3. Add the meat and cook for 5 minutes, or until it loses its red color.

4. Combine the spices, salt and pepper and stir them into the meat mixture.

5. Stir in the tomato paste and water.

6. Lower the heat and simmer for 10 minutes, stirring occasionally.

7. Serve in Soft Corn Tortillas (page 183). Top with Tomato Salsa (page 261), Avocado Dip (page 252) or Guacamole (page 269) and/or grated cheese if desired.

Cook's Note: This recipe can also be made into a burrito by following these instructions: Wrap Soft Corn Tortillas in foil and heat them for 5 minutes in a 400°F oven. Spread each of the warmed tortillas with 2 tablespoons of salsa and 1 tablespoon of sour cream. Add 1 piece of Boston lettuce and top with 2 tablespoons of black beans, 2 tablespoons of grated cheddar cheese and ¼ of the Sloppy Joes recipe. Roll each finished burrito and keep it warm on a tray in the oven while you prepare the remaining burritos. Warm all the finished burritos for a few minutes before serving.

Soft Corn Tortillas

These tortillas are excellent holders for Sloppy Joes. You can also use fully cooled tortillas as sandwich wraps.

Prep time: 15 minutes

Cook time: 20 minutes

Makes: 4 (9-inch) tortillas

¾ cup yellow cornmeal

½ cup potato flour

2 tablespoons tapioca flour

½ teaspoon xanthan gum

½ teaspoon sea salt

1 cup warm water

½ teaspoon honey

1. Place all the ingredients in a medium bowl and stir to combine, until the mixture forms a soft dough.

2. Form the dough into 4 equal-sized balls.

3. Place a piece of plastic wrap on a board and dust the plastic with cornmeal. Place one of the dough balls on the plastic wrap, dust the top-side of the dough ball with cornmeal and cover it with another piece of plastic wrap. Using a rolling pin, roll the dough into a 9-inch circle.

4. Roll out the remaining dough balls, and stack the flattened wraps on a plate or tray, separated by plastic wrap so they don't stick together.

5. Heat a 9- or 10-inch frying pan or griddle (preferably cast iron), or another type of heavy-bottomed pan, over medium-high heat for 5 minutes, or until hot. It should not be too hot, or the tortillas will burn.

6. Before making the first tortilla wipe the hot frying pan or griddle with a folded paper towel soaked in 1 teaspoon of oil.

7. Cook each tortilla for 1 minute per side, or until lightly browned.

8. Stack the cooked tortillas separated by waxed paper.

Sloppy Joes on Soft Corn Tortillas

Greek Ground Lamb Crumble

Serve this lamb crumble on a Soft Pita Wrap topped with Tzatziki Sauce.

Prep time: 20 minutes

Cook time: 12 minutes

Makes: 4 servings

Meat Filling

2 tablespoons extra virgin olive oil

1 medium onion, chopped

1 clove garlic, finely chopped

1 pound ground lamb*

½ teaspoon sea salt

¼ teaspoon freshly ground black pepper

½ teaspoon paprika

½ teaspoon dried oregano

½ teaspoon dried thyme

½ teaspoon dry mustard

1 can (6 ounces) tomato paste

1 cup water

1 recipe Tzatziki Sauce (page 257)

1 recipe Soft Pita Wraps (page 165)

1. Heat the oil in a medium-sized frying pan over medium-high heat for 3 minutes, or until hot.

2. Sauté the onion for 2 minutes, or until it starts to brown.

3. Add the garlic and sauté for 30 seconds.

4. Raise the heat to high and add the lamb. Break up the lamb with a wooden spoon and allow it to cook undisturbed for a few minutes so that it starts to brown; then, cook for 5 minutes.

5. Combine the salt, pepper, paprika, oregano, thyme and dry mustard and sprinkle over the lamb.

6. Stir in the tomato paste and the water and cook for 5 minutes, stirring several times during cooking. If the heat seems to be too high, lower it to medium-high.

7. Spoon the browned meat into the wraps and top each with a dollop of tzatziki.

Substitute ground turkey or beef if you prefer.

Cook's Note: Unless you have a lot of time to prepare this dish, it is highly recommended that you prepare the tzatziki sauce and pita wraps in advance. You can even prepare the meat in advance, and reheat it in a frying pan when you are ready to serve (add a little water while reheating, if needed). If you prepare everything in advance, you can assemble this meal in less than 15 minutes, and everything will taste as good as or better than if you had made it all to order.

Stir-Fried Chicken with Red Peppers and Cashews

Prep time: 25 minutes

Cook time: 10 minutes

....

Makes: 4 servings

....

Marinade

3 cloves garlic, crushed

½ cup **Spicy Ketchup (page 271)**

½ cup **organic tamari sauce**

Chicken

1 pound skinless, boneless, white meat chicken breasts

3-4 tablespoons grapeseed oil

2 red peppers, seeded, cut in half lengthwise and sliced into ½-inch slices

4 scallions, including the white part and 1 inch of the green part, thinly sliced on the diagonal

¼-½ cup water

1 cup cashews

1. Combine the marinade ingredients in a gallon-sized resealable plastic storage bag. Add the chicken and seal well. Allow the chicken to marinate for several hours in the refrigerator.

2. When you are ready to cook the chicken, remove it from the marinade, reserving the marinade for later use. Blot the chicken with a paper towel to remove any excess marinade.

3. Heat half the oil in a heavy duty frying pan until it is very hot and starts to sizzle.

4. Lower the heat to medium-high, add about half of the chicken and stir fry for about 1½-2 minutes, or until it is nicely browned. Remove from the frying pan.

5. Add the remaining chicken, stir fry for 1½-2 minutes and remove.

6. Add the remaining oil. Stir fry the red peppers and the scallions for 2 minutes, or until they are slightly charred.

7. Return the chicken to the frying pan.

8. Add the water to the bag with the remaining marinade and pour the liquid into the pan with the chicken. Stir and cook for 1 minute.

9. Add the cashews and stir well.

10. Serve over cooked brown rice, or with cooked rice vermicelli.

Meatballs and Spaghetti Squash

If you have never had spaghetti squash, you are in for a surprise. It isn't pasta, but it sure looks and tastes like it! Topped with meatballs and Garden Fresh Tomato Sauce, it's a great substitute for the real thing.

Prep time: 20 minutes

Cook time: 1 hour and 10 minutes

Makes: 6 servings and 12 meatballs

Meatballs

1 recipe Garden Fresh Tomato Sauce (page 259)

1 pound ground beef

2 tablespoons cooked quinoa

1 teaspoon onion powder

½ teaspoon garlic powder

½ teaspoon sea salt

¼ teaspoon freshly ground black pepper

2 tablespoons extra virgin olive oil

Squash

1 (4-5 pound) spaghetti squash, halved lengthwise and with seeds removed

2 cups hot water

1. If you have not already made the Garden Fresh Tomato Sauce, do so now.

2. Combine all the meatball ingredients, except for the tomato sauce and the oil, in a medium-sized bowl.

3. Form the meat mixture into 12 (2-inch) meatballs.

4. Heat the oil in a medium-sized frying pan over medium-high heat for 2-3 minutes, or until hot.

5. Add the meatballs to the frying pan and cook for 8-10 minutes, or until well-browned on all sides.

6. Place the tomato sauce in a saucepot to simmer over medium heat.

7. Add the meatballs to the tomato sauce and allow them to cook for at least 1 hour.

8. When you begin cooking the meatballs in the sauce, preheat the oven to 350°F.

9. Place the squash, cut side down, in a dish with sides that is large enough to hold both pieces.

10. Pour 2 cups of hot water into the dish.

11. Bake in the preheated oven for 40-50 minutes, or until a knife inserted in the center of the squash passes easily through the skin.

12. Remove the squash from the pan and allow it to sit for 5 minutes, or until it is cool enough to handle.

13. Using a fork, separate the stringy pulp into spaghetti-like strands and spoon it into a serving bowl.

14. Top with some sauce and meatballs, and serve the extra sauce and meatballs on the side.

Cook's Note: The texture of the cooked squash will be similar to angel hair pasta. If you prefer the texture to be more vegetable-like, take 10 minutes off the cook time.

Honey Battered Chicken

The sauce on this battered chicken has an Asian flavor and can be enjoyed with a stir-fried medley of your favorite vegetables.

Prep time: 10 minutes

Cook time: 15 minutes

....

Makes: 6 servings

....

Battered Chicken
2 eggs

1½ **pounds of chicken, cut into 1½-inch chunks**

1½ **cups Almond Flour (page 236)**

1½ **teaspoons onion powder**

1½ **teaspoons garlic powder**

1½ **teaspoons paprika**

½ **teaspoon freshly ground black pepper**

⅓-¼ **cup grapeseed or safflower oil**

Sauce
3 **tablespoons raw honey**

1 **tablespoon Coconut Milk (page 237)**

2 **tablespoons mustard**

1 **teaspoon tamari**

1. Preheat the oven to 400°F.

2. Beat the eggs in a large bowl.

3. Add the chicken to the beaten eggs.

4. Mix the almond flour, onion powder, garlic powder, paprika and pepper together on a flat plate or tray.

5. Dredge the egged chicken cubes in the flour mixture until they are nicely coated.

6. Heat ¼ cup of the oil in a medium-sized frying pan over medium-high heat for 3 minutes, or until hot.

7. Add half the chicken pieces and cook for 3 minutes per side.

8. Remove the cooked chicken to a heat-proof platter and place in the preheated oven to keep warm.

9. Repeat Steps 7-8 with the remaining chicken.

10. Mix the honey, coconut milk, mustard and tamari in a bowl.

11. Pour the sauce over the cooked chicken and toss until all the pieces are well-coated.

Slow Cooked Vegetarian Tempeh Chili

Prep time: 1 hour 20 minutes (including standing time)

Cook time: 10-12 hours

. . . .

Makes: about 3 quarts

. . . .

1 pound red kidney beans, rinsed

3 tablespoons grapeseed oil

1 large onion, chopped

3 large garlic cloves, chopped

1 red or green pepper, chopped

2 stalks celery, sliced

1 carrot, peeled and chopped

1 (8 ounce) package tempeh

2-3 tablespoons chili powder

1 teaspoon ground cumin

1 teaspoon ground coriander

1 (2-inch) strip of kombu (optional)

1 can (28 ounces) diced tomatoes

3 cups Vegetable Stock (page 235)

1 cup raw fresh corn kernels

1. Place the beans in a 4-quart saucepot and fill the pot with water to a level of at least 3 inches above the beans. Bring to a boil over medium-high heat. Turn the heat off and allow the beans to soak for 1 hour.

2. While the beans are soaking, heat 2 tablespoons of the oil in a large frying pan over medium-high heat for 3 minutes, or until hot.

3. Sauté the onion for 3 minutes, or until it starts to brown.

4. Add the garlic and sauté for 30 seconds.

5. Add the pepper, celery and carrot and sauté for 3 minutes.

6. Spoon the sautéed vegetables into the bowl of a slow cooker.

7. Heat the remaining oil in the frying pan over medium-high heat for 3 minutes, or until hot.

8. Add the tempeh to the frying pan and sauté for 3 minutes, or until browned.

9. Add the sautéed tempeh and all the remaining ingredients, except for the corn, to the slow cooker. Drain the water from the soaked beans and stir them into the slow cooker.

10. Cover the cooker and set it to Cook on Low for 12-14 hours. Stir the corn into the cooker for the last 2 hours of cooking.

11. Serve topped with sour cream and grated cheddar cheese if desired.

Nutrition Note: Originating in Indonesia and now used worldwide in vegetarian cuisine, tempeh has a firm texture and strong flavor. Like tofu, tempeh is made from soybeans, but it has different nutritional characteristics and textural qualities. It's made by a natural culturing and controlled fermentation process that binds the soybeans into a cake form. This fermentation process, and the retention of the whole soybean, gives tempeh a higher protein, dietary fiber and vitamin content than tofu.

Red and Green Pepper Frittata

A frittata is the Italian version of an omelet. It is partially cooked on the stovetop and then finished in the oven.

Prep time: 10 minutes

Cook time: 50 minutes

Makes: 2-3 servings

1 red pepper, seeded and thinly sliced

1 green pepper, seeded and thinly sliced

1 medium red skinned potato, thinly sliced

2 tablespoons extra virgin olive oil, divided

½ teaspoon sea salt

1 teaspoon garlic powder

¼ teaspoon freshly ground black pepper

4 eggs, lightly beaten

1 teaspoon Herbes de Provence

2 tablespoons grated Parmesan, or your favorite permitted cheese

1. Preheat the oven to 400°F.

2. Place the peppers and potato in a single layer on a baking sheet.

3. Pour 1 tablespoon of the oil over the vegetables.

4. Combine the salt, garlic powder and pepper and sprinkle evenly over the vegetables.

5. Toss the vegetables well to coat.

6. Bake in the preheated oven for 40 minutes (stirring once after 20 minutes), or until the potatoes and the edges of the peppers begin to brown.

7. Remove the vegetables from the oven, but leave the oven on.

8. Whisk the eggs, Herbes de Provence and cheese together.

9. Heat the remaining oil in an oven-proof 10-inch frying pan over medium-high heat for 1 minute.

10. Pour the eggs into the hot pan and cook for about 1 minute to allow them to set.

11. Spoon the vegetables over the eggs and cook for 1 minute.

12. Place the frying pan in the hot oven and cook for 7 minutes, or until the top is browned and the eggs are set.

13. Serve the frittata directly in the frying pan, or turn it out onto a large plate.

Cook's Note: Frittatas are a great way to use leftover vegetables. Use this recipe as a template and substitute your favorite cooked vegetables. You can even add cooked turkey sausage, leftover salmon or chicken to the vegetables.

Zucchini Corn Bake

Serve with a salad for a light supper.

Prep time: 20 minutes

Cook time: 35-40 minutes

....

Makes: 4-6 servings

....

2 cups diced, unpeeled zucchini

1½ cups (about 3 ears) fresh corn, cut from the cob

1 small onion, finely chopped

1 teaspoon each freshly chopped parsley and basil

½ teaspoon freshly chopped thyme

3 eggs

2 tablespoons extra virgin olive oil

½ cup Almond Milk (page 237)

½ cup Gluten-Free Baking Mix (page 241)

1 teaspoon garlic powder

½ teaspoon sea salt

¼ teaspoon freshly ground black pepper

½ cup grated Parmesan cheese

½ cup grated cheddar cheese

1. Preheat the oven to 400ºF.

2. Grease an 8x8x2-inch square baking dish.

3. Combine all the ingredients in a large bowl. Stir well to mix completely.

4. Pour the mixture into the prepared baking dish.

5. Bake in the preheated oven for 35-40 minutes, or until a toothpick inserted in the center comes out clean.

Cook's Note: This recipe can be prepped in advance by cooking only partially. Cook for 30 minutes and refrigerate. When you are ready to serve, cover the dish with foil and bake in a 350ºF oven for 10-15 minutes, or until hot.

Mixed Berries with Crème Patisserie (Vanilla Pastry Cream)

Your family and friends will be impressed when you serve this fancy-sounding dessert. No one has to know just how simple it is to make.

Prep time: 10 minutes
Cook time: 8 minutes

Makes: 1 cup

1 cup Almond Milk (page 237)
3 egg yolks
2 tablespoons tapioca flour
2½ tablespoons xylitol
1½ teaspoons vanilla
Assorted berries

1. Heat the almond milk in a small saucepan over medium heat for about 5 minutes, until it scalds, at which time small bubbles will rim the edge of the pan. Remove from the heat.

2. Combine the egg yolks, tapioca flour and xylitol in another small saucepan.

3. Pour 2 tablespoons of the scalded milk into the egg mixture and whisk constantly until combined.

4. Pour in the remaining milk and whisk until combined.

5. Cook over medium heat until the mixture thickens, whisking occasionally.

6. Remove from the heat and stir in the vanilla.

7. Spoon the crème into a bowl and cover with plastic wrap, so that the plastic wrap lies directly on top of the crème.

8. Refrigerate until ready to use. Serve over berries.

PHASE 4 **Variation:** Once you reach Phase 4, you can make this recipe into a delicious pie using the crust found in the Spinach and Sun-Dried Tomato Quiche recipe (page 221). Bake the crust as directed for 10 minutes and allow it to cool completely. Fill the crust with a double recipe of Crème Patisserie and top with assorted berries. Refrigerate the pie for several hours before serving.

Nutrition Note: Blueberries rank number one in fruits that contain antioxidants, and they are also very high in vitamin C.

Watermelon Lime Cooler

This drink could not be easier to make, but it will have everyone asking you for the recipe!

Prep time: 10 minutes

Makes: about 2 cups

2 cups watermelon chunks, seeds removed

1 lime, juiced

1 cup ice cubes

1. Place the ingredients in a blender container. Cover, and blend on High, or on a frozen drink setting.

Cook's Note: This drink is great to serve at a summer barbecue. Blend the watermelon and lime in batches ahead of time. When you are ready to serve, fill a pitcher with crushed ice, pour the juice over the ice and stir. The drink can also be served over cubed ice if desired.

Raspberry Lemonade Slushie

Serve this lemonade over crushed ice to make slushies, or as traditional lemonade in tall glasses over cubed ice. Either way, it's a cooling, delicious drink.

Prep time: 10 minutes
Cook time: 10 minutes

Makes: 1 quart

1 quart water

½ cup xylitol

1 cup raspberries

½ cup lemon juice (juice of 2 lemons)

Finely crushed ice

1. Combine the water, xylitol and raspberries in a saucepan. Bring the water to a boil and boil for 10 minutes, or until the raspberries are reduced to pulp.

2. Remove the saucepan from the heat and strain the liquid through a sieve to remove all the seeds. Discard the seeds.

3. Stir in the lemon juice and refrigerate the drink until ready to serve.

4. Using a blender or ice crusher, crush the ice and scoop it into glasses. Pour the lemonade over the ice and serve.

Cook's Note: Blueberries, blackberries, strawberries or even sliced peaches or mango can be substituted for the raspberries in this recipe.

Lime Ice

This is as simple a recipe as can be, but be sure to begin making the ice early in the day, so that it will be ready when you want to eat it.

Prep time: 5 minutes

Cook time: 10 minutes

Cool time: 2½ hours

....

Makes: 2 cups

....

1½ cups water

¾ cup xylitol

¼ cup lime (or lemon) juice

1. Combine the water and the xylitol in a small saucepan and cook over high heat for about 7 minutes, or until it comes to a boil.

2. Remove from the heat and stir in the juice.

3. Allow to cool over a water bath, or place the mixture in the freezer for 15 minutes to cool.

4. Pour the cooled mixture into a 13x9-inch pan and place it in the freezer.

5. After about 1½ hours, remove the pan from the freezer and scrape the ice with a fork, mixing the more softly-frozen center with the harder edges.

6. Return the pan to the freezer. Repeat the forking process every half hour for about 2 hours, or until the ice is set.

Cook's Note: Substitute lemon juice for lime to make Lemon Ice, or 2 tablespoons of lemon juice and 2 tablespoons of orange juice to make Citrus Ice.

Peach Ice Cream

Make this ice cream at the height of peach season. Plan a trip to the orchard to pick your own, or visit your local farmers' market. Peaches fresh from the tree are an absolute taste treat – far more delicious than those found in the supermarket.

Prep time: 10 minutes

Cook time: 5 minutes

Cool time: 30 minutes

Freeze time: 30 minutes

. . . .

Makes: 1 pint
(4 standard scoops)

. . . .

¾ **cup Almond Milk
(page 237)**

2 tablespoons xylitol

1 egg yolk

**8 ounces fresh or frozen
peach slices**

2 tablespoons water

¼ **cup xylitol**

½ **teaspoon vanilla**

1. Combine the milk and 2 tablespoons of the xylitol in a small saucepan. Cook over medium heat, stirring occasionally, for about 5 minutes, or just until the mixture comes to a boil.

2. While the mixture is cooking, beat the egg yolk with a wire whisk or fork for about 1 minute, or until it lightens in color.

3. Once the mixture boils, remove about 2 tablespoons to a small container. Very slowly, whisk these 2 tablespoons into the egg yolk.

4. Once it is incorporated, whisk the egg yolk mixture into the heated almond milk. Cook, stirring constantly with a wooden spoon, until the mixture thickens to a custard-like consistency that coats the back of the spoon.

5. Place the mixture in the refrigerator to cool for about 30 minutes.

6. Meanwhile, place the peaches, water, ¼ cup of the xylitol and the vanilla in the bowl of a food processor. Pulse about 10 times, until the peaches are chopped, but not liquefied.

7. Combine the peaches and the custard mixture in the bowl of an electric ice cream maker. Follow the instructions that came with your ice cream maker to freeze the ice cream.

8. If the ice cream is not quite hard enough to scoop immediately, place it in the freezer for 30 minutes to firm it up.

Cook's Note: This ice cream is best when eaten the day it's made, so make it the day you want to serve it, if possible. If you don't like peach ice cream, or you want a change, substitute 2 cups of strawberries for the peaches and continue as directed.

Fig and Apricot Cookies

This recipe is an adaptation of an old Italian family favorite that's usually baked at Christmas time.

Prep time: 40 minutes

Standing time: 1 hour 20 minutes

Cook time: 20 minutes

....

Makes: about 20 cookies

....

Dough
¾ cup whole wheat flour

¼ cup oat flour

2 tablespoons tapioca flour

2 tablespoons almond flour

2 tablespoons semolina flour

1 tablespoon potato flour

⅓ cup xylitol

¼ teaspoon sea salt

½ teaspoon vanilla extract

1 egg

⅓ cup margarine

Filling
4 ounces soft, dried mission figs, stems removed

3 ounces (⅓ cup) dried apricots

1 tablespoon Almond Meal (page 236)

3 tablespoons honey

1 tablespoon orange juice

1½ teaspoon ground cinnamon

Egg wash (1 egg and 1 teaspoon water, combined)

1. Place all the dough ingredients in the bowl of a food processor. Cover, and pulse about 15 times, until the mixture is combined and is the texture of coarse sand.

2. Pour the mixture onto a large piece of plastic wrap, and gather up the sides and twist the wrap, so that the dough forms a plastic-wrapped ball. Refrigerate the dough for about an hour.

3. Meanwhile, place all the filling ingredients, except for the egg wash, in the bowl of a food processor. Pulse about 15 times, or until the figs and apricots are chopped and the mixture is combined.

4. Preheat the oven to 350ºF.

5. Dust a 15-inch piece of plastic wrap with whole wheat flour. Place half the dough in the center and place a second piece of plastic wrap over the top of the dough. Using a rolling pin, roll the dough out into an 8- inch rectangle between the layers of plastic.

6. Spoon half of the filling into a stripe running down the center of the dough.

7. Pick up one edge of the plastic wrap and use it to fold the dough over the filling. Continue rolling the dough until you have a log-shaped roll.

8. Use the remainder of the dough to make a second log in the same way as above.

9. Refrigerate both logs for about 20 minutes.

10. Remove the logs from the refrigerator and slice each into 10 pieces.

11. Line a baking sheet with parchment paper and place the sliced cookies so that they are standing up as if still in the loaf.

12. Paint the tops of the cookies with the egg wash.

13. Bake for 20 minutes until they are lightly browned.

Roasted Banana Ice Cream

Roasting the bananas brings out the natural sweetness of the fruit, allowing you to use less honey in this ice cream recipe.

Prep time: 30 minutes

Cook time: 25 minutes

Cool time: 30 minutes

Freeze time: 30 minutes

Makes: about 2 cups
(4 standard scoops)

3 very ripe bananas

1 teaspoon vanilla

¾ cup Almond Milk
(page 237)

3 tablespoons honey or
xylitol

1 egg yolk

1. Preheat the oven to 425°F.

2. Place the bananas in a baking dish. Roast in the preheated oven for 20 minutes, or until the skins blacken and start to split.

3. Carefully remove the bananas from the skins and place the bananas in the bowl of a food processor, along with any of the syrupy liquid that has cooked out of the bananas. Add the vanilla.

4. Meanwhile, heat the milk and honey or xylitol in a small saucepan over medium-high heat, stirring occasionally, for about 5 minutes, or until the mixture comes to a boil.

5. While the mixture is cooking, beat the egg yolk with a wire whisk or fork for about 1 minute, or until it lightens in color.

6. When the mixture comes to a boil, remove about 2 tablespoons and very slowly whisk into the egg yolk.

7. When the milk and egg yolk are fully incorporated, whisk them into the remainder of the heated milk and cook, stirring constantly with a wooden spoon, for about 8 minutes, or until the mixture thickens to a custard-like consistency that coats the back of the spoon.

8. Place the mixture in the food processor with the bananas and process for about 20 seconds.

9. Refrigerate the mixture for about 30 minutes.

10. Place the cooled mixture in the bowl of an electric ice cream maker. Follow the instructions that came with your ice cream maker to freeze the ice cream.

11. If the ice cream is not quite hard enough to scoop immediately, place it in the freezer for 30 minutes to firm it up. The ice cream is best if used within a few days.

Green Apple Ice

Green apples are tart and crisp — a great fruit to make into an ice.

Prep time: 2½ hours
(including freeze time)

Makes: about 1 quart

1½ **cups water**

¾ **cup xylitol**

2 **large green apples,
peeled, cored and cut
into pieces**

1. Combine the water and the xylitol in a small saucepan and cook over high heat for about 7 minutes, or until it comes to a boil.

2. Remove from the heat and allow to cool for about 15 minutes.

3. Place the apples and about half of the cooled syrup in the blender, and blend until the apples are pureed.

4. Pour the blended apple mixture back into the saucepot with the remainder of the syrup, and mix well.

5. Pour the mixture into a 13x9-inch pan and place it in the freezer.

6. After about an hour, remove the pan from the freezer and scrape the ice with a fork, mixing the more softly-frozen center with the harder edges.

7. Return the pan to the freezer. Repeat the forking process every half hour for about 1 hour, or until the ice is set.

Cook's Note: Ices are best when eaten the day they are made. If they stand in the freezer for too long, they will harden and not be as appealing.

Pumpkin-Cranberry Muffins, page 211

Phase 4
Contents

Seared Peppered London Broil (page 179) with Roasted Vegetables (page 171)

Phase 4: The Maintenance Phase *(six months to indefinite)*

Phase 4 of the Lyme Inflammation Diet® begins eight weeks after you began Phase 1. Although Phase 4 provides you with more food choice options than do Phases 1-3, your goal in Phase 4 is to continue to consume only foods and beverages that are healthy. Should you still be experiencing symptoms of chronic inflammation, remain on the earlier Phases of the diet until your symptoms subside before moving on to Phase 4. Once you do begin this Phase, strictly abide by the guidelines below for at least six months to ensure that you obtain the most benefit. If at all possible, you should permanently avoid the poor quality UNIT foods, such as fried foods and refined sugar.

By the time you begin Phase 4, you should be able to determine which healthy foods you can enjoy without triggering inflammation, and which foods you should permanently avoid. After six months of following Phase 4, you may begin to occasionally reintroduce some of the foods to which you were previously sensitive (not allergy-triggering foods, which should only be added after clearance from your physician), but these foods should still only be consumed once a week or less, if at all. A good rule of thumb is, "If in doubt, leave it out."

Phase 4 includes all the foods and beverages you safely consumed during the first three Phases, plus new selections listed below.

Foods Allowed During Phase 4

Fruits
Grapes (purple) [1]
Kiwi [1]
Papaya [1]
Raisins[1] NEW

Nuts/Seeds
Hemp seeds

Vegetables
All other pickles NEW
Parsnips NEW
Radishes
Red potatoes
Scallions

Turnips
Watercress
Yams

Grains
Whole wheat flour

Protein Sources
Cod NEW
Grouper NEW
Pork[2] NEW
Shellfish [2] NEW

Herbs/Spices
Horseradish NEW

Dairy
Feta
Unsweeted kefir

Fats
Peanut oil

Other
Chocolate (unsweetened, with 70% or greater cocoa content)
Gelatin NEW
Yeast NEW

---

[1] Use sparingly, as they are very high in sugar.

[2] These are not ideal foods and should be eaten rarely – no more than once a week.

Whole Grain Waffles with Assorted Berries

In this final Phase, whole wheat flour can be added to your diet. These whole grain waffles are higher in nutritional value than waffles made from white flour, and they are every bit as delicious. Try topping them with berries and maple syrup, or, for an extra berry boost, with homemade Blueberry or Raspberry Syrup (page 255).

Prep time: 15 minutes

Cook time: 20 minutes

Makes: about 4 waffles

1 cup whole wheat flour

¼ cup millet

¼ cup spelt flour

2 teaspoons baking powder

½ teaspoon sea salt

½ teaspoon cinnamon

1 tablespoon xylitol

1 egg, slightly beaten

⅓ cup Ghee (page 234) or melted margarine

1½ to 1¾ cups Almond Milk (page 237)

1 teaspoon vanilla

Assorted berries, such as blueberries, blackberries and raspberries

1. Preheat the waffle maker.

2. Combine the dry ingredients in a medium-sized mixing bowl.

3. Combine the wet ingredients and whisk them into the dry ingredients. Initially, add 1½ cups almond milk; then, if the mixture is still too thick, add another ¼ cup.

4. Follow the instructions that came with your waffle maker to bake the waffles.

5. Top the finished waffles with an assortment of your favorite berries, and maple or homemade berry syrup.

PHASE 3 Variation: To make Gluten-Free Waffles, use 1 cup Gluten-Free Baking Mix (page 241), 1 cup almond milk, 1 egg, ⅓ cup ghee or melted margarine and ½ teaspoon vanilla, and follow the mixing directions in this recipe. Cook the waffles until brown and crisp.

Cook's Note: Mornings are busy, so why not make the batter the night before and refrigerate it? That way, everyone can make their own waffles whenever they're ready for them. You can also make the waffles ahead of time, refrigerate or freeze them, and then reheat them in a toaster or toaster oven.

Breakfast Burritos

Make the wraps and measure out the ingredients the night before, and the next morning, you'll be eating your breakfast burritos in 20 minutes!

Prep time: 15 minutes

Cook time: 10 minutes

Makes: 4 servings

1 recipe Soft Pita Wraps (page 165)

1 cup Tomato Salsa (page 261)

½ cup sour cream

½ cup canned black beans, drained

1 cup shredded cheddar cheese, divided

1 tablespoon butter

8 eggs

1. Preheat the oven to 350ºF.
2. Place the wraps in foil and warm them in the preheated oven while you assemble the ingredients.
3. Remove the wraps from the oven and top each with a quarter of the salsa, sour cream and black beans, and with 2 tablespoons of the cheese.
4. Heat the butter in a medium-sized frying pan.
5. Add the eggs to the pan and cook for 30 seconds, until they are set.
6. Scatter the remaining cheese over the eggs and scramble with a fork. Cook until set.
7. Spoon equal amounts of the cooked eggs over each of the wraps.
8. Roll the wraps, place them on a baking tray and return them to the oven.
9. Heat for 5 minutes, or until warm, and serve.

Cook's Note: Now that you've reached the final Phase of the diet, you will have identified which foods trigger problems. At this point, you may begin returning foods to your diet that you know are not triggers. Therefore, you may use commercially-made tortillas and salsa for this recipe, if you prefer not to make your own. Read the labels to ensure they do not contain any ingredients not allowed in the LID.

Pumpkin-Cranberry Muffins

Pumpkin and cranberries appear in the market at about the same time of year. They're a winning combination in these muffins, which make a great autumn breakfast.

Prep time: 15 minutes
Cook time: 20 minutes

Makes: 6 muffins

¾ cup canned, or cooked and pureed, pumpkin

¼ cup Cran-Raspberry Sauce (page 256)

3 tablespoons extra virgin olive oil

1 egg, beaten

2 tablespoons honey

¼ cup maple syrup

½ teaspoon vanilla

¾ cup whole wheat flour

2 tablespoons tapioca flour

2 tablespoons oat flour

1 teaspoon baking powder

1 teaspoon baking soda

1 teaspoon ground cinnamon

¼ teaspoon ground ginger

¼ teaspoon sea salt

½ cup chopped pecans or walnuts

1. Preheat the oven to 400ºF.

2. Grease a 6-cup muffin pan and set it aside.

3. Combine the pumpkin, cran-raspberry sauce, oil, egg, honey, syrup and vanilla in a medium-sized bowl.

4. Combine the remaining ingredients, except for the nuts, and stir this flour mixture into the pumpkin mixture.

5. Stir in the nuts.

6. Fill each muffin cup with a scant ½ cup of batter.

7. Bake in the preheated oven for 20-22 minutes, or until a toothpick inserted in the center of a muffin comes out clean.

Whole Wheat Banana Raisin Bread

Prep time: 20 minutes

Cook time: about 1 hour (including roasting bananas)

....

Makes: 1 loaf

....

2 large ripe bananas

½ cup old fashioned oats

2 eggs

1 teaspoon vanilla

¼ cup honey or xylitol

½ cup safflower oil, Ghee (page 234) or melted margarine

1 cup whole wheat flour

¼ cup Almond Meal (page 236)

1 teaspoon baking powder

1 teaspoon baking soda

¼ teaspoon sea salt

¼ cup raisins or chopped walnuts

1. Preheat the oven to 425ºF.

2. Grease an 8x8x2-inch loaf pan.

3. Place the bananas, with skins on, on a baking sheet and bake in the preheated oven for 20 minutes.

4. Remove the bananas from the oven and allow to cool slightly.

5. Lower the oven temperature to 350ºF.

6. Remove the skins and mash the bananas. Place the mashed bananas, along with any liquid that accumulated on the baking tray, into a bowl.

7. Add the oats, eggs, vanilla and honey and oil mix well.

8. Allow the mixture to stand for about 10 minutes, to soften the oats.

9. Meanwhile, combine the flour, almond meal, baking powder, baking soda and salt, and stir into the banana mixture.

10. Stir in the raisins or nuts.

11. Spoon the dough into the greased loaf pan and bake in the 350ºF oven for 40-45 minutes, or until a toothpick inserted in the center comes out clean.

Cook's Note: The batter for this recipe can be made into 6 muffins, rather than a loaf. To make muffins, preheat the oven to 400ºF and bake for 15-20 minutes, or until a toothpick inserted in the center of a muffin comes out clean.

No Knead Whole-Grain Sandwich Thins

These easy-to-make sandwich thins are delicious with Slow Cooked Pulled Chicken (page 217).

Prep time: 20 minutes
Rise time: about 5 hours
Cook time: 25 minutes

Makes: 1 dozen

1 tablespoon yeast
4 cups lukewarm (105°F) water
1 teaspoon honey
2 tablespoons extra virgin olive oil
6 cups whole wheat flour
½ cup cornmeal
½ cup millet **flour**
½ cup semolina flour
1 teaspoon sea salt
2 tablespoons sesame seeds

1. Dissolve the yeast in ¼ cup of the water and stir in the honey. Allow it to stand for 5 minutes, or until it is bubbling.

2. Stir the oil into the remaining water and set aside.

3. Combine the flours and salt in a large (3-quart) bowl. Stir well.

4. Stir the risen yeast and all but ½ cup of the water into the flour mixture. Using a wooden spoon, stir until all the flour is moistened, adding the remaining ½ cup of water if needed. The dough will be quite loose.

5. Oil a piece of plastic wrap and place it loosely over the bowl, oiled side down. Allow the dough to rise in a draft-free place for 2-5 hours.

6. When the dough has risen to the top of the bowl, divide the dough in half and then divide each half into 6 equal-sized pieces.

7. Dust a board liberally with whole wheat flour. On the floured board, roll each piece of dough into a ball.

8. Line 2 baking sheets with parchment paper.

9. Place the sesame seeds on a flat plate, and then press each dough ball into the seeds.

10. Place the dough balls on the baking sheets, leaving an inch of space on all sides of each ball. Place the sheets in a draft-free place and cover them with a clean towel. Allow the thins to rise for 1½ hours.

11. Preheat the oven to 425°F and bake the thins in the preheated oven for 25-30 minutes, or until they are nicely browned.

12. Place the thins on a cooling rack for about 20 minutes before serving.

Cook's Note: The dough can also be used to make two loaves of bread. Grease two 8-inch loaf pans, divide the dough in half and place it in the pans. Allow the loaves to rise in a draft-free place for 2 hours, or until the dough has risen over the tops of the pans. Bake in the preheated oven for 25-30 minutes, or until the loaves are well-browned and sound hollow when tapped with a knife.

Cream of Tomato Bisque

Whether you have a bumper crop of tomatoes in your garden, or you get them from your farm share or farmers' market, nothing beats tomatoes at the peak of their season. Have this soup for lunch, or with salad for a light dinner on a cold night.

Prep time: 20 minutes

Cook time: 35 minutes

....

Makes: 6 servings
(about 5 cups)

....

1 tablespoon extra virgin olive oil

2 tablespoons chopped shallots (about 1 large shallot)

2 cloves garlic, chopped

2 pounds fresh ripe tomatoes

2 tablespoons tomato paste

1 tablespoon freshly chopped parsley

1 tablespoon freshly chopped basil

1 teaspoon sea salt

1 teaspoon honey

1 teaspoon dried Herbes de Provence or Italian seasoning

½ teaspoon freshly ground black pepper

1¼ cups Chicken Stock (page 240)

¾ cup heavy cream

1 tablespoon freshly chopped basil (for garnish)

1. Heat the oil in a 3-quart saucepot.

2. Sauté the shallot over medium heat for 2 minutes, or until it starts to brown.

3. Add the garlic and sauté for 30 seconds.

4. Add all the remaining ingredients, except for the heavy cream and the basil. Bring the soup to a boil, then lower the heat to medium and simmer for 20 minutes.

5. Strain the soup into a bowl and reserve the liquid.

6. Place the contents of the strainer in a blender container or the bowl of a food processor, and blend or puree until smooth.

7. Return the reserved tomato liquid to the saucepot, and add the pureed solids and heavy cream.

8. Bring the soup to a simmer over medium heat.

9. As soon as the soup simmers, it is ready to serve. Sprinkle with chopped basil if desired.

Slow Cooked Pulled Chicken

Slow cooking is every working person's best friend. After a long, hard day, what could be more pleasing than to walk into a house filled with the delicious aroma of BBQ?

Prep time: 15 minutes

Cook time: 9 hours 20 minutes

. . . .

Makes: about 2 quarts

. . . .

2 tablespoons extra virgin olive oil

6 large chicken thighs with skin (4 pounds)

1 large onion, chopped

4 cloves garlic, pressed

3 cups Spicy Ketchup (page 271)

1 tablespoon chili powder

1-2 tablespoons raw apple cider vinegar

¼ cup honey

2 tablespoons mustard

1 teaspoon ground cumin

½ teaspoon sea salt

1 teaspoon celery salt

1 teaspoon paprika

1. Heat the oil in a large frying pan over high heat for 3 minutes, or until hot.

2. Lower the heat to medium-high, add the chicken, and brown it on the skin side for 8-10 minutes, or until well browned. Turn the chicken thighs and cook for 5 minutes.

3. Remove the chicken from the pan to cool.

4. Add the onion and garlic to the pan and sauté for about 3 minutes, or until limp and just starting to brown.

5. Remove the skin from the chicken and discard.

6. Place the sautéed onions and the remaining ingredients in a slow cooker and stir well.

7. Add the skinned chicken. Cover the cooker, and set it to Cook on Low for 7-9 hours.

8. Remove the chicken from the cooker and, using 2 forks, shred the meat and discard the bones.

9. Return the chicken to the pot and stir well. Serve on No Knead Whole-Grain Sandwich Thins (page 214), or with corn bread.

Cook's Note: Brown the chicken with the skin on, because the rendered fat from the skin adds lots of flavor. Remove the skin before adding the chicken to the slow cooker, because the added fat is not desirable in the finished dish. You can do all the prep for this recipe the night before and store the ingredients in the refrigerator. Then, all that's left to do in the morning is to add the ingredients to the slow cooker and turn it on. You can't overcook this recipe – the longer it cooks, the better it tastes! The recipe makes a lot by design; it's a great choice for a party, or a "pot luck supper," or even just an everyday meal. Leftovers reheat well, and can even be frozen for future use.

Chicken Tamaki

Tamaki is a type of hand-rolled, cone-shaped sushi that's easy for a sushi beginner to make and eat. This version is comprised of cooked brown rice, stir-fried chicken, carrot and cucumber, with a tasty dipping sauce.

Prep time: 15 minutes

Cook time: 5 minutes

....

Makes: 8 rolls

....

Marinade/Dipping Sauce

¼ cup tamari

¼ cup Spicy Ketchup (page 271)

2 tablespoons water

1 teaspoon mustard

½ teaspoon sesame oil

2 teaspoons honey

½ teaspoon wasabi (optional)

8 ounces skinless chicken breast, cut into thin strips

2 tablespoons safflower oil

Rolls

4 sheets nori (dried seaweed), cut in half horizontally

⅓ cup cooked brown rice

1 carrot, peeled and cut into thin strips

1 cucumber, cut into thin strips

1. Combine all the marinade/dipping sauce ingredients, except for the chicken and the oil, and divide the mixture in half.

2. Pour half the sauce into a quart-sized resealable plastic bag. Pour the remaining sauce into a small serving bowl for dipping, and set aside. Add the chicken to the bag with the marinade. Seal the bag and refrigerate it for up to an hour.

3. Heat the oil in a medium-sized frying pan for 3 minutes, or until hot.

4. Remove the chicken from the plastic bag. Stir fry the chicken in the hot oil for 2-3 minutes, or until nicely browned.

5. Lay a piece of nori on a cutting board. Spread 1 tablespoon of cooked rice over the nori. Place a piece of the cooked chicken, a carrot stick and a cucumber spear on top of the rice. Starting at one end, roll the nori so that it makes a cone-shaped roll with the filling inside.

6. Repeat the above step to make the remainder of the rolls.

7. Serve with the dipping sauce on the side.

Nutrition Note: Wasabi is a plant best known for its spicy root. Grated wasabi root tastes like strong horseradish and is commonly served with sushi. It is very low in cholesterol and sodium and is a good source of vitamins B6 and C, calcium, magnesium, potassium, manganese and dietary fiber.

Whole Wheat Pizza Dough

This whole wheat dough is great for Vegetable Whole Wheat Pizza (page 222), or for any of your other favorite pizzas.

Prep time: 15 minutes
Rise time: 2 hours 45 minutes

....

Makes: 1 thick-crust pizza dough, or 2 thin-crust pizza doughs

....

1½ cups lukewarm (105°F) water

¼ teaspoon honey

1 package (5⁄16 ounce) active dry yeast

2-2½ cups whole wheat flour

1½ cups semolina flour

1 teaspoon sea salt

1 tablespoon extra virgin olive oil

1. Combine the water, honey and yeast in a bowl and stir well to combine. Cover the bowl and place it in a warm place for about 10 minutes, or until the yeast bubbles and starts to grow.

2. Meanwhile, combine all the remaining ingredients, except for the oil, in a large mixing bowl.

3. Add the proofed yeast and the oil to the flours and stir well to incorporate.

4. Using a mixer with a dough hook, knead the bread dough for 10 minutes. You can also knead by hand for 10 minutes if desired.

5. Remove the dough from the mixing bowl. Grease the bowl with a small amount of extra virgin olive oil. Return the dough to the bowl.

6. Cover the dough with a clean cloth and place it in a warm, draft-free place to rise for 2 hours, or until it has doubled in bulk.

7. Remove the dough from the bowl and punch it down (see Cook's Note below). Return the dough to the bowl, cover and allow it to rise again for 45 minutes to an hour.

8. If you are not using the dough immediately, refrigerate or freeze it until you are ready to use it.

Cook's Note: If you prefer thin-crust pizza, divide the dough in half after the first rise. Oil another bowl, put half the dough in each and cover both bowls with a clean towel. Allow the dough to rise again for 45 minutes, or until it has again doubled in bulk.

Spinach and Sun-Dried Tomato Quiche

The whole wheat crust in this quiche stands up well to the bold taste of the spinach and sun-dried tomatoes.

Prep time: 30 minutes

Cook time: 50 minutes

Makes: 6-8 servings

Crust

½ cup butter or margarine, cut into small pieces

1 cup whole wheat flour

¼ cup oat flour

¼ teaspoon sea salt

2-4 tablespoons ice-cold water

Filling

2 tablespoons extra virgin olive oil

1 large shallot, finely chopped

2 cloves garlic, finely chopped

⅓ cup chopped sun-dried tomatoes, packed in olive oil

1 bag (6 ounces) baby spinach, finely chopped (about 3 cups)

½ teaspoon sea salt

¼ teaspoon freshly ground black pepper

1 cup Almond Milk (page 237)

4 eggs

¼ teaspoon sea salt

⅛ teaspoon freshly ground black pepper

1 cup grated sharp cheddar

½ cup grated Parmesan cheese

1. Place the butter or margarine in the freezer for about 30 minutes. Combine the flours and salt in a food processor.

2. Scatter the butter over the flour. Pulse several times until the butter is cut into the flour.

3. With the food processor running, slowly pour the ice-cold water down the feed tube and process until the dough just begins to form a ball. Add the water slowly, so as not to add too much.

4. Form the dough into a ball and wrap it in plastic warp. Refrigerate for about 30 minutes.

5. Preheat the oven to 400°F.

6. Line a board with waxed paper and lightly dust the paper with flour. Place the dough on the paper, lightly flour the top of the dough and roll it into a 10-inch circle.

→ *Prebake crust 10 min*

7. Meanwhile, heat the oil in a large frying pan over medium heat for 2 minutes, or until hot.

8. Add the shallot and garlic and sauté for 2 minutes.

9. Add the sun-dried tomatoes and sauté for 1 minute.

10. Add the spinach, salt and pepper and sauté for 1 minute, or until just limp. Allow the mixture to cool slightly.

11. Combine the milk, eggs, salt, pepper and cheeses in a large bowl and mix well.

12. Add the spinach mixture to the milk and egg mixture and stir well.

13. Pour the filling into the pre-baked crust and bake for 35 minutes, or until the top is nicely browned and a knife inserted 1 inch from the center of the quiche comes out clean.

Vegetable Whole Wheat Pizza

This is about the healthiest pizza you could ever make, and it tastes delicious. If you do not like some of the suggested toppings, replace them with the toppings of your choice.

Prep time: 25 minutes
Cook time: 20 minutes

Makes: 8 slices

1 tablespoon extra virgin olive oil, divided

½ large red pepper, seeded and cut into strips

1 medium onion, sliced into rings

2 cloves garlic, crushed

4 mushrooms, quartered

¼ teaspoon each salt and pepper

1 recipe Whole Wheat Pizza Dough (page 219)

1 tablespoon corn meal

2 tablespoons Mixed Herb Pesto (page 141)

½ cup tomato sauce

1 can (14 ounces) artichoke hearts, drained and quartered

½ cup green and gaeta olives, pitted and cut in half

12 cherry tomatoes, cut in half

2 tablespoons freshly grated Romano or Parmesan cheese

1. Place a pizza stone or cast iron pizza pan in a cold oven, and then heat the oven to 550ºF.

2. Meanwhile, heat the oil in a medium-sized frying pan for 2 minutes, or until hot.

3. Sauté the red pepper and onion for about 5 minutes, or until the pepper is limp.

4. Add the garlic, mushrooms, salt and pepper and sauté 2 minutes.

5. Stretch the pizza dough to fit the pizza stone or pan. After the stone or pan is fully heated,* carefully remove it from the oven and sprinkle it with the corn meal. Carefully place the dough on the hot pan.

6. Spread the pesto over the dough.

7. Spread the tomato sauce over the dough.

8. Top the pizza with the sautéed vegetables and the remaining ingredients.

9. Carefully place the pizza back in the oven and cook for 20 minutes, or until the crust is nicely browned on the edges and the bottom.

Caution: The stone or pan will be extremely hot and must be handled with good quality oven mitts. The easiest and safest place to put the hot pan while you are assembling the pizza is on the stovetop grate.

Cook's Note: Preheating the pizza stone or pan before cooking the pizza will make the crust pizza-parlor-crispy.

Chicken Croquettes

These croquettes are a tasty way to use up leftover chicken or turkey. Serve them with Cran-Raspberry Sauce (page 256).

Prep time: 20 minutes

Cook time: 15 minutes

. . . .

Makes: 8 croquettes

. . . .

12 ounces cooked chicken or turkey, cut into 2-inch pieces

1 small onion, quartered

1 small carrot, peeled and quartered

2 sprigs parsley

1 clove garlic

½ cup cream

1 egg, beaten

1 large potato, peeled, boiled and mashed

½ teaspoon sea salt

¼ teaspoon freshly ground black pepper

1 tablespoon grated Parmesan cheese

1 cup Italian Breadcrumbs (page 244), divided

2 tablespoons grapeseed or extra virgin olive oil

1. Place the chicken in the bowl of a food processor and pulse 5-6 times, until the chicken is chopped, but not pureed. Remove the chopped chicken to a large mixing bowl.

2. Place the onion, carrot, parsley and garlic in the food processor and pulse until the vegetables are finely chopped.

3. Remove the chopped vegetables to the mixing bowl with the chicken and stir well.

4. Combine the cream, egg, potato, salt, pepper, cheese and ⅓ of the breadcrumbs, and stir the mixture into the chicken and vegetables.

5. Pour the remaining breadcrumbs on a flat plate.

6. Form the mixture into eight 4-inch ovals and roll them in the breadcrumbs.

7. Heat the oil in a large frying pan over medium-high heat for 3 minutes, or until hot.

8. Cook the croquettes for about 8-10 minutes, turning them so that they brown on both sides and all edges.

Cook's Note: You can prepare the croquettes in advance, and cook them later. This will save you time on a busy work day.

Peanut Butter Cookies, page 226

Oatmeal Coconut Raisin Cookies, page 227

Truffle "Brownie" Cake Bars, page 231

Peanut Butter Cookies

Delicious and nutritious: how many cookies can you say that about?

Prep time: 10 minutes

Cook time: 13 minutes

Makes: 12 (3-inch) cookies

¾ cup organic natural peanut butter

¼ cup organic butter, cut into pieces

¼ cup xylitol

1 egg

1 teaspoon vanilla extract

¾ cup spelt flour

¼ cup unsweetened coconut

2 tablespoons ground flaxseed

¼ teaspoon xanthan gum

1 teaspoon baking soda

¼ teaspoon sea salt

1. Preheat the oven to 375ºF.

2. Place the peanut butter, butter, xylitol, egg and vanilla in a large mixing bowl. Using an electric mixer, beat the mixture for 2 minutes.

3. Combine the remaining ingredients, add them to the mixing bowl and mix on Low for about 30 seconds, or until just combined.

4. Using a ¼-cup measuring cup, portion out 12 cookies. Form each portion into a ball and place them on an ungreased cookie sheet, leaving about 1 inch of space around each.

5. Use the tines of a fork to flatten the cookies and make a criss-cross pattern on the top.

6. Bake the cookies in the preheated oven for 12 minutes, or until just lightly browned.

7. Allow the cookies to cool for a few minutes on the baking sheet before transferring them to a cooling rack.

Cook's Note: This recipe has been tested five times using different flours and brands of peanut butter. The texture of the cookie very much depends on the peanut butter used; it varies from soft to crispy to somewhere in between. The dough might be crumbly, but when you gather it in your hands and roll it into a ball, it should have a texture similar to fudge. When you flatten the dough balls with a fork, gather up any loose crumbs and press them back into the cookie to round out the shape.

Oatmeal Coconut Raisin Cookies

Oatmeal raisin cookies are always popular. This version adds unsweetened coconut, and replaces the usual brown and white sugars with maple syrup and agave nectar, making this family favorite into a healthier alternative.

Preheat oven 350°

Prep time: 15 minutes

Cook time: 13-15 minutes

Makes: 12 (3-inch) cookies

½ cup organic butter, cut into 4 pieces

½ cup honey

1 egg

2 tablespoons maple syrup

1 teaspoon vanilla

1 cup organic old fashioned oats

½ cup unsweetened coconut

3 tablespoons Almond Meal (page 236)

2 tablespoons oat flour

¼ cup tapioca flour

2 tablespoons potato flour

¼ teaspoon xanthan gum

1 teaspoon cinnamon

1 teaspoon baking soda

½ teaspoon sea salt

1/3 cup raisins

1. Place the butter, honey, egg, syrup and vanilla in a mixing bowl. Using an electric mixer, mix on High for 2 minutes.

2. Combine the remaining ingredients, except for the raisins, and add them to the mixing bowl, mixing on Low until just combined.

3. Stir in the raisins.

4. Using a standard ice cream scoop, measure 12 portions of batter onto a large baking sheet, leaving at least 1 inch of space around each cookie.

5. Using your palm, press the cookies lightly, to slightly flatten them into 3½-inch rounds.

6. Bake in the preheated oven for 13-15 minutes, or until the cookies are lightly browned.

7. Allow the cookies to cool for a few minutes on the baking sheet and then transfer them to a cooling rack to cool completely.

8. Store the cookies in a tin or cookie jar.

Rice Pudding

Rice pudding is the ultimate comfort dessert. This version uses leftover brown rice, which gives the pudding a nutty flavor and chewy texture.

Prep time: 10 minutes
Cook time: 30 minutes

. . . .

Makes: 4 servings

. . . .

1½ cups cooked brown rice

2 cups Almond Milk (page 237)

⅓ cup xylitol

2 tablespoons melted butter or Ghee (page 234)

⅓ cup raisins

1 teaspoon vanilla extract

1 teaspoon cinnamon

1. Combine the rice, almond milk, xylitol, butter or ghee and raisins in a medium-sized saucepan. Cook the mixture over medium-high heat for about 10 minutes, or until it starts to bubble.

2. Stir the pudding, lower the heat to medium and cook for 20 minutes, or until most of the liquid is absorbed.

3. Remove from the heat and stir in the vanilla and half of the cinnamon.

4. Spoon the pudding into serving dishes and dust with the remaining cinnamon.

Cook's Note: If you like runnier rice pudding, stir in a little more almond milk before serving.

Truffle "Brownie" Cake Bars

Prep time: 15 minutes

Cook time: 20-25 minutes

....

Makes: 9 brownies

....

Brownies
2 eggs

½ teaspoon sea salt

1 cup xylitol

1 teaspoon vanilla extract

1 stick butter, cut into 8 pieces

3 ounces unsweetened chocolate, chopped

¼ cup oat flour

¼ cup coconut flour

¼ teaspoon xanthan gum

½ teaspoon baking soda

Ganache Frosting
¼ cup cocoa powder

½ cup heavy cream

2 tablespoons raw honey

1. Preheat the oven 350ºF.

2. Combine the eggs, salt and xylitol in a large mixing bowl, and beat with an electric mixer for about 3 minutes, or until the eggs are thick and pale yellow in color.

3. Add the vanilla and beat for 30 seconds.

4. Place the butter and chocolate in a microwave-safe bowl and microwave on high for 1-1½ minutes (check after 1 minute to see if the additional time is needed). Stir the chocolate to ensure it's fully melted.

5. With the mixer running, pour the melted chocolate mixture into the egg mixture.

6. Combine the remaining ingredients, add them to the bowl and beat for 30 seconds. Scrape the sides of the bowl and beat for 30 seconds.

7. Grease the bottom of an 8x8x2-inch square baking pan. Spoon the brownie mixture into the pan.

8. Bake in the preheated oven for 20-25 minutes, until the center has just set (a toothpick inserted in the center will come out gooey).

9. Remove the pan from the oven and allow the brownies to cool.

10. When the brownies have fully cooled, combine all the ingredients for the ganache frosting. Mix until thoroughly incorporated.

11. Spread the frosting evenly over the top of the brownies.

12. Place the pan in the freezer for at least 1 hour.

13. Remove the brownies from the freezer and slice while still frozen. Allow the brownies to defrost before serving.

Pantry Contents

Homemade Baking Powder, page 238   Amaranth Flour, page 242   Spicy Rub, page 243

Italian Breadcrumbs, page 244   Ghee, page 234   Almond Butter, page 238

Ghee

Ghee is another name for clarified butter. Clarified butter is the clear yellow liquid that is left after the milk solids have been removed from butter.

Prep time: 5 minutes

Cook time: 45 minutes

. . . .

Makes: about 1½ cups

. . . .

1 pound unsalted organic butter

1. Preheat the oven to 250°F.
2. Place the butter in an oven-proof dish[A].
3. Bake in the preheated oven for 45 minutes. Foam will form on the surface[B], and the milk solids will sink to the bottom of the dish.
4. Remove the pan from the oven and carefully skim off and discard the foam[C].
5. Ladle the clear liquid into a container[D]. Cover and refrigerate for future use.
6. Discard the milk solids[E].

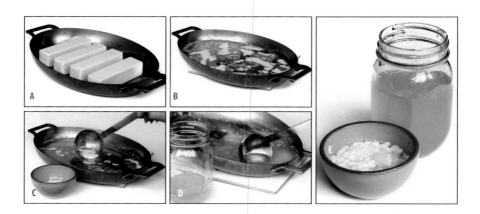

Safety Note: Although pure clarified butter/ghee does not need to be refrigerated, we recommend you store your ghee in the refrigerator because some milk solids may still be present, which can cause the ghee to become rancid. Use ghee in recipes as you would use regular butter (tablespoon for tablespoon).

Nutrition Note: During the clarification process, the milk proteins are removed, making the ghee virtually free of lactose. This makes it a relatively safe alternative for those who are lactose intolerant.

Vegetable Stock

Use this stock as a base for vegetarian soups, or in other recipes that call for stock or broth, such as Lentil Soup (page 122). Vegetable stock can always be substituted for chicken or beef stock. Stock can also be substituted for wine in many recipes.

Prep time: 15 minutes

Cook time: 2 hours

....

Makes: 1½ quarts

....

2 tablespoons extra virgin olive oil, divided

1 large onion, chopped

4 cloves garlic, chopped

2 leeks, well rinsed and chopped

3 carrots, peeled and chopped

3 stalks celery, chopped

1 cup fresh chopped spinach

2 tablespoons chopped chives

4 ounces green beans

12 sprigs parsley

1 teaspoon chopped rosemary

2 sprigs thyme

2 teaspoons sea salt

1 teaspoon garlic powder

3 quarts filtered water

1. Heat the oil in a 6-quart saucepot or stockpot over medium-high heat for 2 minutes, or until hot.

2. Sauté the onion, garlic and leeks in the oil for 7 minutes.

3. Add the remaining ingredients, and bring the soup to a boil. Reduce the heat and simmer for 2 hours.

4. Place a strainer or colander in a 5-quart pot or bowl. Pour the soup and vegetables into the strainer. Press the vegetables with the back of a large spoon, mashing them into puree. Scrape the puree from the sieve into the bowl of stock. This will thicken the stock and add flavor to the broth.

....

PHASE 3 **Variation:** Once you reach Phase 3, you may add 2 large, chopped tomatoes to the recipe for even more flavor.

....

Almond Meal

Prep time: 5 minutes

Makes: about ½ cup

½ cup whole, unblanched raw almonds

1. Place the almonds in an electric coffee grinder.* Pulse the grinder several times until the almonds are ground to a medium-fine texture. Don't over-grind, or you will end up with nut butter.

2. Position a fine sieve over a bowl, and empty the almond meal into the sieve. Work the meal with a spoon until it has all passed through the sieve. If any large pieces remain, grind them again, and return them to the sieve.

3. Use the almond meal in recipes that call for almond meal or almond flour.

   * If you don't have a coffee grinder, you can use a food processor, but the texture will not be as fine.

Almond Flour

Prep time: 15 minutes

Additional time: 1 hour

Makes: 1 cup

1 cup whole, raw almonds
Filtered water

1. Preheat the oven to 170ºF.

2. Place the nuts in a large bowl. Boil the water, pour it over the nuts and allow to stand for 1 minute.

3. Strain the nuts in a colander and rinse with very cold water for 30 seconds.

4. Drain the nuts and spread them on a clean dish towel. Fold the towel over the nuts and rub back and forth until the skins come off.

5. Place the skinless nuts on a baking sheet and cook in the preheated oven for 30 minutes.

6. Allow the nuts to cool for 20 minutes.

7. Using a food processor or coffee grinder, process the nuts until they reach a flour-like consistency.

Cook's Note: Be careful not to process the almond meal or flour too long, or you will end up with nut butter. Refrigerate any unused portions of flour and meal, as it could become rancid if left out. You may substitute hazelnuts, pecans or walnuts to make alternate flours.

Almond Milk

Once you taste a few of the recipes that use almond or coconut milk in place of cows' milk, you will discover that you can easily live without dairy.

Prep time: 15 minutes

Makes: 3½ cups

3½ cups hot water, divided
1½ cups Almond Meal
(page 236)

1. Heat the water in a small saucepan over medium heat until it simmers.
2. Place the almond meal in a blender container and add 3 cups of the hot water.
3. Blend for 2-3 minutes. The mixture will be very thick.
4. Line a colander or a sieve with cheesecloth. Pour the almond mixture into the cheesecloth to strain out the milk. Squeeze out all of the liquid from the mixture into the bowl.
5. Return the pulp to the blender and add ½ cup of the hot water.
6. Repeat steps 3 through 4.

Coconut Milk

Prep time: 10 minutes

Makes: 1½ cups

1½ cups water
1 cup unsweetened
coconut

1. Heat the water in a small saucepan over medium heat until it simmers.
2. Place the coconut in a blender container and add 1 cup of the hot water.
3. Blend for 2-3 minutes. The mixture will be very thick.
4. Line a colander or a sieve with cheesecloth. Pour the coconut mixture into the cheesecloth to strain out the milk. Squeeze out all of the liquid from the mixture into the bowl.
5. Return the pulp to the blender and add ½ cup of the hot water.
6. Repeat steps 3 through 4.

Cook's Note: No dairy products are allowed in the first two Phases of the diet, so almond or coconut milk is used in place of cows' milk. Because these milks are made fresh and have no preservatives, they will last for about 5 days in a sealed container in the refrigerator.

Almond Butter

Nothing could be easier to make than nut butter. All you need is a cup of nuts and a food processor or coffee grinder.*

Prep time: 5 minutes

Makes: ½ cup

1 cup roasted almonds
¼ teaspoon sea salt

1. Place the almonds and salt in the bowl of a food processor. Pulse 10 times, or until the nuts are chopped.
2. Process continually for 2 minutes.
3. Turn off the processor, scrape the sides, and continue to process until the mixture is the consistency of butter.
4. Refrigerate.

   If you are using a coffee grinder, grind no more than ½ cup at a time.

Cook's Note: If the butter is not quite smooth enough for you, add 1 tablespoon of extra virgin olive oil or avocado oil to the mixture, and continue to process for a couple of minutes until the mixture is smoother.

Homemade Baking Powder

Most commercial baking powders contain cornstarch, which is not permitted in the first two Phases of this diet. Making your own baking powder enables you to make the recipes for baked goods found in Phase 2.

Prep time: 2 minutes

Makes: 1 teaspoon

¾ teaspoon cream of tartar
¼ teaspoon baking soda

1. Combine the ingredients.

Cook's Note: Use in recipes that call for baking powder. This recipe makes 1 teaspoon; if you need more, double the amounts.

Cashew Honey Butter

Adding honey to the nuts in this recipe makes a sweet spread. Put it on bananas, apples or pears for an enjoyable and nutritious snack.

Prep time: 5 minutes

Makes: ½ cup

1 cup lightly salted cashews

1 tablespoon raw honey

1 tablespoon extra virgin olive oil

1. Place all the ingredients in the bowl of a food processor. Pulse 10 times, or until the nuts are chopped.

2. Process continually for 2 minutes.

3. Turn off the processor, scrape the sides, and continue to process until the mixture is the consistency of butter.

4. Refrigerate.

Cook's Note: Use this recipe as a template and substitute any permitted nut to make your favorite nut butter.

Chicken Stock

You may wonder why this recipe advises roasting the chicken and vegetables before adding them to the stockpot. Roasting intensifies the flavors, and more flavorful stock makes for more flavorful recipes.

Prep time: 15 minutes

Cook time: 4 hours

Makes: 4½ quarts

4 pounds chicken thighs

4 stalks celery, cut into 3-inch pieces

4 carrots, cut into quarters

4 leeks, cleaned, and with green tops removed

1 onion, cut into quarters

1 head garlic, cut in half

6 ripe plum tomatoes

1 teaspoon sea salt

½ teaspoon freshly ground black pepper

6 quarts water

4 sprigs thyme

8 sprigs parsley

4 sprigs oregano

1. Preheat the oven to 400ºF.

2. Place all the ingredients, except for the herbs and water, in a roasting pan. Roast in the preheated oven for 1½-2 hours.

3. Transfer the roasted chicken and vegetables to an 8-quart saucepot or stockpot. Add the water and herbs, and bring the soup to a boil over high heat. Reduce the heat to medium, and simmer for 2 hours.

4. Allow the stock to cool for about 30 minutes. Remove the chicken from the bones, and save for future use. Strain and discard the vegetables.

5. Refrigerate the broth, and/or freeze any unused portions in small containers for future use.

Cook's Note: You can make beef stock by substituting 4 pounds of beef bones for the chicken in this recipe.

Nutrition Note: Ever wonder why so many moms give chicken soup to their sick children? Soups made from stocks not only facilitate the growth of cells in the gut lining, but can also aid in decreasing inflammation.

Gluten-Free Baking Mix

Preparing this baking mix in advance will save you time, as it is used in several of the recipes in Phases 3 and 4 (such as the Gluten-Free Blueberry Lemon Muffins on page 159).

Prep time: 5 minutes

Makes: about 4¼ cups

1 cup sorghum flour

1½ cups oat flour*

½ cup Almond Meal (page 236)

½ cup tapioca flour

¼ cup potato flour

¼ cup ground flaxseed

4 tablespoons baking powder

2 teaspoons guar or xanthan gum**

1 teaspoon sea salt

1. Combine all the ingredients and store in a sealed container for up to 2 weeks.

2. Keep refrigerated. Use in any recipe that calls for Gluten-Free Baking Mix.

According to the experts at www.celiac.com, recent research indicates that oats may be safe for people on gluten-free diets, although many people may also have an additional, unrelated intolerance to them. Cross- contamination with wheat is also a factor that you need to consider before choosing to include oats in your diet. People with celiac disease should ensure that the oat flour they use is certified gluten-free.

** See page 59 of the LID Food Glossary to learn the difference between guar gum and xanthan gum.*

Cook's Note: It is especially important to keep this mix refrigerated if you use your own home-ground almond meal in the recipe. Almonds and other nuts have a high fat content and these fats can become rancid. Refrigerating the mix will avoid this problem.

Millet Flour

Millet is used in this recipe, but you could just as easily grind amaranth, barley, oats or any other grain by following the same instructions. Just substitute the grain of your choice, and follow these very easy directions.

Prep time: 5 minutes

Makes: ½ cup

½ **cup millet**

1. Place the millet* in an electronic coffee grinder. Grind continuously until all the grain is reduced to a fine flour.

2. Refrigerate any leftover flour in an airtight container.

   * *Depending on which grain is ground, this recipe may be appropriate for Phase 2, 3 and/or 4, so be sure to consult the allowable foods in the beginning of each Phase.*

Cook's Note: If your recipe calls for a larger amount of flour, grind more in ½ cup portions; do not put more than ½ cup of grain in the coffee grinder at a time.

Millet and amaranth have a bitter flavor, which you will notice if you buy millet or amaranth flour commercially. This bitter flavor can be lessened by first soaking the grains for 10 hours. After soaking, rinse and drain and place on a baking sheet. Dry in a 200°F oven for a couple of hours, or until completely dry. Once dry, follow the above directions.

Spicy Rub

Rubs can be used on chicken and fish, as well as on steaks and chops. This spicy version will add zip to any roasted or broiled meat.

Prep time: less than 5 minutes

....

Makes: ½ cup

....

¼ cup paprika

2 tablespoons chili powder

2 teaspoons dry mustard

2 teaspoons ground cumin

2 teaspoons xylitol

2 teaspoons coarse sea salt

½ teaspoon dried oregano

½ teaspoon dried thyme

½ teaspoon freshly ground black pepper

1. Combine all the ingredients in a small jar or covered container.

Cook's Note: This rub will keep for 3 months when stored in a covered jar or container in your pantry. The recipe can be halved or doubled.

Italian Breadcrumbs

Use any leftover bread or No Knead Whole-Grain Sandwich Thins (page 214) to make these delicious breadcrumbs. Store them in an airtight container, and use in any recipe that calls for breadcrumbs.

Prep time: 10 minutes

Cook time: 45 minutes

. . . .

Makes: ¾ cup

. . . .

6 ounces No Knead Whole-Grain Sandwich Thins (page 214), cut into 1-inch cubes

1 teaspoon garlic powder

1 teaspoon onion powder

1 teaspoon Italian seasonings

½ teaspoon sea salt

¼ teaspoon freshly ground black pepper

1 tablespoon grated Parmesan cheese

1. Preheat the oven to 225ºF.

2. Place the bread cubes in the bowl of a food processor fitted with a steel blade. Pulse until the bread is reduced to fine crumbs.

3. Spread the crumbs in a thin layer on a sheet pan. Bake for 45 minutes, or until the crumbs are dry.

4. Return the crumbs to the food processor and process until they are evenly, finely ground.

5. Remove to a bowl and combine with the remaining ingredients.

Cook's Note: This recipe can be doubled or tripled if you have a large amount of leftover bread to use up. The breadcrumbs will keep for over a month if stored in an airtight container.

Croutons

Leftover bread can be used to make these croutons. Allow them to cool, and then store them in an airtight container.

Prep time: 5 minutes

Cook time: 35 minutes

. . . .

Makes: about 3 cups

. . . .

½ teaspoon onion powder

1 teaspoon Herbes de Provence

8 ounces allowable bread, cut into ¾-inch cubes

3 tablespoons extra virgin olive oil

1 tablespoon grated Parmesan cheese

1. Preheat the oven to 350°F.

2. Combine the onion powder and Herbes de Provence in a bowl.

3. Toss the bread cubes in the herbs and cheese until coated.

4. Add the oil to the bowl and toss until the bread cubes are coated.

5. Place the bread cubes on a small baking sheet and bake in the preheated oven for 35 minutes. Carefully turn them midway through cooking to ensure even baking.

6. Cool completely before serving or storing.

Cook's Note: These croutons can be made from any bread allowable on the LID. Use them to top salads or soups.

Blueberry Syrup, page 255   Orange Herb Dressing, page 266   Peachy Barbeque Sauce, page 263

Sauces & Condiments Contents

Homemade Mayonnaise

Basic mayonnaise can be turned into a flavorful spread with the addition of some simple ingredients. As indicated, most of the Variations are permitted in Phase 1.

Prep time: 15 minutes

Makes: about 1 cup

1 egg and 1 egg yolk, room temperature

½ teaspoon sea salt

1½ tablespoons raw apple cider vinegar

¾ cup extra virgin olive oil or virgin olive oil
(see Cook's Note on page 249)

1. Place the eggs, salt and vinegar in a blender container. Cover, and blend on High for 30 seconds.

2. With the blender running, remove the center of the lid. Very slowly (this should take about 1½-2 minutes), drizzle the oil in a steady stream into the opening until the sauce forms an emulsion and thickens.

3. Remove the mayonnaise from the blender. Keep refrigerated.

PHASE 1 Variations:

Herb Mayonnaise: Stir 1-2 tablespoons of your favorite freshly chopped herbs, such as basil, oregano, rosemary, dill, chives or any combination, into the Homemade Mayonnaise.

Curried Mayonnaise: Stir ½-1 teaspoon of curry powder into the Homemade Mayonnaise.

Pesto Mayonnaise: Stir 2 tablespoons of Mixed Herb Pesto (page 141) into the Homemade Mayonnaise.

PHASE 4 Variation:

Mustard Mayonnaise Dressing: Stir 1 tablespoon of mustard into the Homemade Mayonnaise.

Cook's Note: Mayonnaise can be made in a food processor, but it will be thinner than commercial mayonnaise. However, it will thicken somewhat when refrigerated.

Garlic-Shallot Mayonnaise (Aioli)

Prep time: 20 minutes

Makes: about 1 cup

1 egg and 1 egg yolk, room temperature

1 small clove garlic

½ small shallot, cut in half

½ teaspoon sea salt

½ teaspoon raw honey

1½ tablespoons raw apple cider vinegar

¾ cup extra virgin olive oil or virgin olive oil

1. Place all the ingredients, except for the oil, in a blender container. Cover, and blend on High for 30 seconds.

2. With the blender running, remove the center of the lid. Very slowly (this should take about 2 minutes), drizzle the oil in a steady stream into the opening until the sauce forms an emulsion and thickens.

3. Remove the mayonnaise from the blender. Keep refrigerated.

PHASE 3 **Variation:** To make Sun-Dried Tomato Aioli, add 2 tablespoons of sun-dried tomatoes to the blender with the shallots and garlic, and proceed as directed above.

Cook's Note: Extra virgin olive oil has a strong flavor. When you reach Phase 3, experiment with some of the more neutral-flavored oils, such as sunflower seed oil or safflower oil. All oils are a one-to-one substitution. If using these oils, be sure to check their labels for "expeller pressed," which ensures that no chemicals were used in pressing the seeds to make the oil.

Cinnamon Applesauce

Green apples are the only apples permitted in Phase 1. They are available year-round and make wonderful applesauce. Why not make a batch and take some to work for a snack?

Prep time: 10 minutes

Makes: 2½ cups

2 pounds green apples (about 4 large apples), peeled and cut into 1-inch pieces

⅔ cup water

½ teaspoon cinnamon

⅛ teaspoon sea salt

2-3 teaspoons raw honey

1. Combine all the ingredients, except for the honey, in a 2-quart saucepot. Bring the mixture to a boil over medium heat. Cover the pot, and lower the temperature to medium. Cook for about 20 minutes, or until the apples soften and begin to fall apart.

2. Remove the sauce from the heat and allow it to cool for about 15 minutes before stirring in the honey.

3. Applesauce can be served warm or cold. Refrigerate or freeze any leftovers.

Cook's Note: This recipe can be doubled or cut in half.

Zabaglione Sauce

If company is coming and you have no idea what to serve for dessert, make this easy sauce and serve it over berries or any seasonal fruit. You can even make it in advance to save time.

Prep time: 5 minutes
Cook time: 10 minutes

....

Makes: about ¾ cup

....

4 egg yolks
1 tablespoon xylitol or
~~agave nectar~~ raw honey
2 tablespoons Almond
  Milk (page 237)
½ teaspoon vanilla extract

1. Whisk all the ingredients in the top section of a double boiler (see Cook's Note).

2. Fill the bottom section of the boiler with about 1 inch of hot water. Cook for about 5 minutes or until it simmers, over medium heat. Do not allow the water to boil.

3. Place the top section of the boiler over the simmering water. Be careful not to let the water in the bottom section touch the top section in which the sauce is being cooked. If the water touches the top section, the egg will curdle or scramble.

4. Cook, whisking constantly, for about 3 minutes, or until the sauce thickens to a pudding-like consistency. Remove the top section of the double boiler from the heat and remove the sauce to a bowl to cool.

....

PHASE 3 **Variation:** Once you reach Phase 3, you may add some lemon juice and lemon zest to the recipe.

....

Cook's Note: If you do not have a double boiler, use a saucepan and a bowl that fits over the pan without touching the contents.

Warning: If you see small lumps forming while you whisk the sauce, remove the top section from the heat immediately and whisk the sauce vigorously. Lumps can form if the water is too hot, or if it touches the bottom of the top section. You will be able to save your sauce if you catch it in time and whisk constantly until it is smooth. Remove the finished sauce from the top section as soon as you finish whisking, as the heat stays in the metal and can cause the sauce to curdle.

Avocado Dip

This dip is a snap to make. In Phase 1 of the diet, use it as a dip for carrots and celery.

Prep time: 5 minutes

Makes: about 2 cups

2 ripe avocados, skinned, pitted and cut into cubes

1 small clove garlic

1 tablespoon chopped chives

⅓ cup Homemade Mayonnaise (page 248)

¼ teaspoon sea salt

½ teaspoon sesame oil

1. Place all the ingredients in a blender container. Cover, and blend on High until smooth.

PHASE 3 **Variation:** Once you reach Phase 3, you can add some lime juice and ground cumin, and serve this dip with Sloppy Joes (page 182) and Soft Corn Tortillas (page 183).

Béarnaise Sauce

See the recipe for Poached Eggs Florentine with Béarnaise Sauce on page 74.

Prep time: 10 minutes

Makes: about ¾ cup

2 egg yolks

1 teaspoon chopped tarragon or lemon thyme

½ tablespoon raw apple cider vinegar

⅓ cup Ghee (page 234)

1. Place all the ingredients, except for the ghee, in a blender container and blend on High for 30 seconds.

2. With the blender running, slowly drizzle the ghee into the container until it forms an emulsion.

3. Remove the sauce from the container and use immediately, or refrigerate until ready to use.

Cook's Note: Béarnaise sauce, like mayonnaise, can be made in a food processor rather than a blender, but it will be thinner than Béarnaise sauce made from commercial mayonnaise. However, it will thicken somewhat when refrigerated.

Mango Dressing

This salad dressing is perfect over salad topped with broiled, blackened or grilled fish, such as Cran-Raspberry Glazed Salmon (page 135). It can also dress any mixed fruit salad.

Prep time: 5 minutes

Makes: 1 cup

1 ripe mango, peeled and diced

2 tablespoons raw apple cider vinegar

1 tablespoon raw honey

2 teaspoons maple syrup

1 tablespoon orange juice *pineapple*

¼ teaspoon sea salt

⅛ teaspoon freshly ground black pepper

⅛ teaspoon each onion powder and garlic powder

¼ cup extra virgin olive oil

1. Place all the ingredients, except for the oil, in the bowl of a food processor. Cover the processor, and process until the mango is completely liquefied.

2. Pour the oil down the feed tube and process for 30 seconds.

3. Refrigerate.

PHASE 3 variation: Once you reach Phase 3, you may add ½ lemon, juiced and zested. Place the lemon in the food processor along with the other ingredients in Step 1.

Cook's Note: When you zest a lemon, be careful not to include any of the white layer (pith) on the underside of the lemon's skin, as it is very bitter. A lemon's zest has more flavor than its juice because all the essential oils are in the skin.

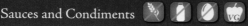

Blueberry Syrup

Most commercial syrups are made with corn syrup and other additives, but this syrup is mostly blueberries. The result is a syrup so pure, it tastes like eating liquid blueberries. Pour it over pancakes, waffles or even ice cream.

Prep time: 10 minutes

Cook time: 15 minutes

Makes: about ½ cup

1 pint fresh blueberries, rinsed and with stems removed

½ cup water

⅓ to ½ cup xylitol

1 teaspoon raw apple cider vinegar

½ teaspoon vanilla

1. Place all the ingredients, except for the vanilla, in a blender container. Blend on High until liquefied.

2. Pour the mixture into a 3-quart or larger saucepot. (If you use a smaller pot, the syrup might boil over while it is cooking.)

3. Heat the mixture over high heat for about 1 minute, or until it comes to a boil. Lower the heat to medium and simmer for 10 minutes. The mixture will begin to bubble and form a layer of foam during the first 10 minutes of cooking.

4. Skim all the foam off the surface and discard. You will be left with clear syrup.

5. Remove the syrup from the heat and stir in the vanilla.

6. Allow the syrup to cool for about 30 minutes before using or storing. Store any unused portions in a glass jar or container, and refrigerate for up to 3 weeks.

Cook's Note: This recipe can be doubled, but be sure to use a 5- to 6-quart saucepot to avoid boil over.

To make Raspberry Syrup, substitute raspberries for blueberries and reduce the water to ¼ cup. Continue as directed above. When using raspberries, you must strain the cooked syrup through a sieve to remove the seeds. If the syrup seems too thin after removing the seeds, return it to the saucepot, bring it to a boil over high heat and cook for 2 minutes, or until it thickens slightly. The syrup will thicken a bit more as it cools.

Berry Pear Sauce

This sauce is very versatile. Use it to top pancakes or crepes, or serve it alongside roast chicken.

Prep time: 10 minutes
Cook time: 10 minutes

....

Makes: 4 servings

....

1 ripe pear, peeled and cut
   into thin slices
½ cup raspberries
½ cup blackberries
⅓ cup water
2 teaspoons xylitol

1. Combine all the ingredients in a small saucepan. Cook over medium heat for 5 minutes.
2. Remove the fruit to a serving bowl. Raise the heat, and bring the syrup to a boil. Cook for 5 minutes, or until the liquid is the consistency of maple syrup.
3. Serve over Oat Crepes (page 115).

....

PHASE 3 Variation: Once you reach Phase 3, you may substitute peaches for the pears and/or strawberries for the raspberries.

....

Cook's Note: When pears are not in season, you can substitute apples. If fresh berries are not available, substitute frozen.

Cran-Raspberry Sauce

Make plenty of this tasty sauce when you reach Phase 2 – you will find it in several recipes in Phases 2 and 3. In addition to the recipes that call for it, this sauce is also a great accompaniment to poultry dishes.

Prep time: 5 minutes

....

Makes: about 3½ cups

....

1 cup water
1 bag (12 ounces) fresh or
   frozen cranberries
1 cup frozen raspberries
½ cup xylitol

1. Place all the ingredients in a 2-quart saucepan. Cover the pan, and cook over medium-high heat until the liquid begins to boil. Lower the heat to medium-low and simmer for 10 minutes.
2. Refrigerate the sauce until ready to use.

Cook's Note: Cranberries are seasonal, but they freeze very well, so buy a few bags to freeze and use year-round. Leave them in their original, unopened bags, and place each bag in a freezer zip-top bag for extra protection against freezer burn.

Tzatziki Sauce

This yogurt cucumber sauce is a perfect side dish, salad dressing, or topping for Greek Ground Lamb Crumble (page 184) with Soft Pita Wraps (page 165).

Prep time: 20 minutes

Standing time: 1 hour

. . . .

Makes: about 1½ cup

. . . .

2 cups peeled, seeded and finely chopped cucumbers (1 large or 2 medium cucumbers)

½ teaspoon sea salt

¼ teaspoon freshly ground black pepper

½ teaspoon extra virgin olive oil

½ teaspoon raw apple cider vinegar

½ small garlic clove, crushed

1 teaspoon dried onion flakes

1 teaspoon freshly chopped mint (optional)

1 (6 ounce) container plain Greek yogurt

1. Place the cucumbers in a bowl, sprinkle them with the salt and toss well to coat.

2. Place the salted cucumbers in a strainer positioned over a bowl. Allow the cucumbers to stand and drain for about 30 minutes.

3. Place the cucumbers between some paper towels, or in a clean dish towel, and squeeze out any remaining liquid.

4. Combine the remaining ingredients and stir well.

5. Add the cucumbers to the mixture, and allow to stand in the refrigerator for at least 1 hour before using.

Cook's Note: If you can make the tzatziki the night before, or even several hours before you plan to serve it, the flavors will have time to blend together.

Easy Oven-Roasted Marinara Sauce

Cooking marinara sauce in the oven might sound funny, but it works, and it saves you the trouble of sautéing onions and garlic (not to mention of cleaning up a messy stove-top).

Prep time: 10 minutes

Cook time: 45 minutes

Makes: about 2 cups

1 can (28 ounces) whole tomatoes, chopped, or 2 pounds vine-ripened tomatoes, chopped

2 tablespoons extra virgin olive oil

1 medium onion, peeled and chopped

2 cloves garlic, thinly sliced

1 teaspoon dried oregano

½ teaspoon sea salt

¼ teaspoon freshly ground black pepper

1-2 teaspoons honey

2 teaspoons balsamic vinegar

1 tablespoon freshly chopped parsley

8 large basil leaves, cut into strips

1. Preheat the oven to 425°F.

2. Place the chopped tomatoes on a baking sheet. Add all the remaining ingredients, except for the parsley and basil, and toss well to combine. Spread the mixture out into a thin layer.

3. Put the baking sheet in the oven and roast for 30 minutes, or until the tomatoes begin to caramelize and most of the liquid has cooked off.

4. Stir in the chopped parsley and basil, and roast for 15 more minutes.

5. The sauce will be very thick and chunky. If thinner, smoother sauce is desired, puree the mixture in a blender or food processor.

6. Serve the sauce immediately over pasta (add a little pasta water to thin, if desired), use it for pizza or refrigerate it for future use.

Cook's Note: This sauce is great on Vegetable Whole Wheat Pizza (page 222).

Garden Fresh Tomato Sauce

Tomatoes fresh from the garden or farm stand can't be beat. This recipe makes a large batch of sauce, so one session in the kitchen will give you enough for several meals. The sauce also freezes very well.

Prep time: 20 minutes

Cook time: 1 hour 10 minutes

Makes: about 3 quarts

1 large or 2 medium onions, quartered

6 cloves garlic, peeled

2 tablespoons extra virgin olive oil

6 pounds fresh ripe tomatoes

2 tablespoons freshly chopped parsley

2 tablespoons freshly chopped basil

2 teaspoons dried oregano

1 teaspoon sea salt

½ teaspoon freshly ground black pepper

1-2 tablespoons raw honey

1. Place the onions and garlic in a food processor and pulse about 8 times, or until the onion is finely chopped.

2. Heat the oil in a 5-quart saucepot over medium-high heat for 3 minutes, or until hot.

3. Sauté the onions for 5 minutes, or until they start to brown.

4. While the onions cook, process the tomatoes in batches in a food processor, pulsing about 10 times for each batch, or until the tomatoes are pureed.

5. Pour the pureed tomatoes into the saucepot.

6. Add all the remaining ingredients, except for the honey. Bring the mixture to a boil over medium-high heat. Reduce the heat to medium and simmer for 1 hour.

7. Remove from the heat and allow the sauce to cool before stirring in the honey.

8. Store the sauce in the refrigerator until ready to use, or freeze it in serving-sized containers for future use.

Nutrition Note: Tomatoes are rich in the powerful antioxidant, Lycopene. Cooking them releases the Lycopene from the plant's cells and increases the body's ability to absorb it.

Fruit Salsa

This blend of summer fruits makes a perfect salsa to serve with broiled fish or chicken.

Prep time: 15 minutes

Makes: about 2 cups

2 scallions, white part only, chopped (1 cup)

1 large peach, peeled and chopped (1 cup)

½ cup freshly chopped pineapple

½ ripe mango, peeled and chopped (about ¾ cup)

2 teaspoons chopped jalapeño pepper

¼ teaspoon garlic powder

¼ teaspoon sea salt

¼ teaspoon pepper

1 teaspoon extra virgin olive oil

¼ lime, juiced

1 1-inch slice of ginger, quartered

¼ teaspoon raw honey

1. Combine all the ingredients in a mixing bowl.

2. Allow the salsa to stand at room temperature for 30 minutes, to allow the flavors to blend.

Cook's Note: When these summer fruits are not available, you can substitute an orange for the peach, and a peeled and sliced pear for the mango.

Tomato Salsa

Everyone loves salsa. Enjoy it as a dip, or as a topping for Sloppy Joes (page 182). Serve the Sloppy Joes on Soft Corn Tortillas (page 183) for an easy Mexican meal.

Prep time: 20 minutes

Makes: 2 cups

1½ pounds cherry or Roma tomatoes, chopped

1 stalk celery, chopped

1 tablespoon chopped jalapeño pepper

2 chopped scallions, white part only

1 clove garlic, crushed

½ lime, juiced

1 teaspoon cumin

½ teaspoon sea salt

¼ teaspoon freshly ground black pepper

¼ teaspoon raw honey

2 tablespoons chopped cilantro or parsley

1 tablespoon freshly chopped basil

1. About 1 hour before serving time, combine all the ingredients in a small mixing bowl.

2. Allow the salsa to stand at room temperature for about 30 minutes before serving. Refrigerate any leftover salsa.

Cook's Note: This versatile salsa can be made with fresh tomatoes when they are at the height of their season, or with chopped, canned tomatoes during the rest of the year. Be sure to remove the seeds from the jalapeño pepper, and *never* touch your eyes or skin after handling these or any hot peppers. If possible, wear disposable gloves while chopping peppers.

Spicy Tangerine BBQ Sauce

Tangerines are an under-used citrus fruit, but this unique BBQ sauce puts them to good use. The miso gives it a slightly Asian flavor, and it pairs very well with chicken.

Prep time: 20 minutes
Cook time: 25 minutes

....

Makes: about ½ cup

....

1 teaspoon extra virgin olive oil

3 scallions, white part only, chopped

1 clove garlic, pressed

⅓ cup Spicy Ketchup (page 271)

1 tablespoon raw apple cider vinegar

1 teaspoon freshly chopped thyme

½ teaspoon ground cumin

¼ teaspoon dry mustard

¼ teaspoon sea salt

½ teaspoon freshly grated ginger

1 tangerine, zested and juiced

½ teaspoon sesame oil

1 tablespoon raw honey or xylitol

1 tablespoon miso

1. Heat the oil over medium-high heat in a 1-quart saucepan for 2 minutes, or until hot.

2. Sauté the scallions for 2 minutes, or until limp.

3. Add the garlic and sauté for 1 minute.

4. Combine the remaining ingredients, except for the honey or xylitol and the miso, and add to the saucepan.

5. Bring the sauce to a boil. Lower the heat and simmer for 15 minutes.

6. Remove the saucepan from the heat and allow the sauce to cool to 115°F before adding the honey or xylitol and miso.

7. Pour the sauce into a storage container and refrigerate until ready to use.

Cook's Note: In most of the country, tangerines are a seasonal fruit. Prepare an extra recipe or two of this sauce and freeze it to use in those months when tangerines are not available.

Peachy Barbeque Sauce

Sweet peaches, spicy ketchup and a kick of chili powder make this barbecue sauce great for broiled meats, or as a burger topping. Try mixing it with some Herb Mayonnaise (page 248) for a sandwich spread.

Prep time: 15 minutes

Cook time: 17 minutes

. . . .

Makes: about 1½ cups

. . . .

4 ripe peaches, peeled and cubed

1 cup Spicy Ketchup (page 271)

1 tablespoon raw apple cider vinegar

1 teaspoon lemon juice

1 tablespoon orange juice

1 teaspoon mustard

1 teapoon onion powder

½ teaspoon paprika

½ teaspoon sea salt

½-1 teaspoon chili powder

¼ teaspoon freshly ground black pepper

1-2 tablespoons raw honey

1. Combine all the ingredients, except for the honey, in a food processor, and process until smooth.

2. Pour the mixture into a saucepot. Cover the pot, and cook over high heat for about 2 minutes, or until the sauce just boils. Lower the heat to medium, and cook for about 15 minutes, or until the sauce thickens.

3. Allow the sauce to cool to 115°F before stirring in the honey.

4. Refrigerate any leftover sauce for future use.

Cook's Note: If you like your sauces spicy hot, add a full tablespoon of chili powder (or more). You can also intensify the heat after cooking by adding extra chili powder and simmering for 15 more minutes.

Miso Barbecue Sauce

Miso is a fermented soy product that can be used in soups and sauces. This sauce has a distinctly Asian flavor and can be used as a marinade or barbecue sauce.

Prep time: 15 minutes

Makes: ¾ cup

2 tablespoons miso

¼ cup water

1 1-inch piece ginger, cut into quarters

1 clove garlic, cut in half

3 scallions, white part only, cut into 3 pieces each

¼ teaspoon pepper

1 tablespoon raw apple cider vinegar

1 teaspoon sesame oil

2 tablespoons Spicy Ketchup (page 271)

2 tablespoons raw honey

1 tablespoon safflower oil

1 tablespoon tamari

1. Place all the ingredients in a blender container. Cover, and blend on High until smooth.

2. Use as a marinade for chicken, turkey or fish.

Cook's Note: Never reuse a marinade, or pour it over cooked food. If you want to baste your cooked dish with the marinade, marinate your dish in ½ cup of the marinade and reserve the rest for basting, or for serving as a sauce with the meal. Also, if you do serve marinade as a sauce with the meal, heat it to boiling before serving.

Mustard Ranch Dressing

Use this dressing for salad, as a dip for fresh cut vegetables or spread it on chicken or fish before broiling or baking.

Prep time: 5 minutes

....

Makes: ½ cup

....

½ **cup Herb Mayonnaise (page 248)**

2 **tablespoons cows' milk kefir**

½ **teaspoon mustard**

¼ **teaspoon garlic powder**

¼ **teaspoon sea salt**

¼ **teaspoon freshly ground black pepper**

1. Combine all the ingredients in a small bowl.
2. Refrigerate any leftover portion.

Cook's Note: This recipe can be doubled. The dressing can be refrigerated for up to 3 weeks.

Orange Herb Dressing

Orange is a delightful flavor variation on a classic vinaigrette dressing. Toss with your favorite greens and top with dried fruits, such as chopped figs, dates or cranberries, and nuts.

Prep time: 10 minutes

Makes: about ½ cup

2 tablespoons raw apple cider vinegar

1 tablespoon raw honey

¼ cup orange juice

1 small clove garlic, crushed

1½ teaspoons mustard

¾ teaspoon Herbes de Provence

¼ teaspoon sea salt

⅛ teaspoon pepper

⅓ cup extra virgin olive oil

1. Combine all the ingredients in a jar or container with a lid. Cover, and shake for 30 seconds, or until the oil thoroughly combines with the other ingredients.

2. Serve over your favorite salads, or use as a marinade for chicken or fish. ·

Cook's Note: For a change of pace, marinate chicken or fish in this dressing for up to 30 minutes before broiling.

Peach and Pineapple Dipping Sauce

Serve this sauce with Coconut Chicken Tenders (page 139), or with any other poultry dish.

Prep time: 10 minutes

Cook time: 30 minutes

....

Makes: about 1½ cups

....

2 ~~peaches~~ *pears*, peeled and chopped *(can be ~~canned~~)*

1 cup fresh, chopped pineapple

⅓ cup orange juice or orange mango juice

¼ teaspoon garlic powder

⅛ teaspoon sea salt

1 tablespoon raw honey

1. Place all the ingredients, except for the honey, in a small saucepan. Cook over high heat for about 5 minutes, or until the mixture comes to a boil. Cover the pan, and lower the heat to medium. Cook for about 15 minutes, or until the fruit breaks down and the mixture thickens.

2. Break up the fruit with a large spoon, and continue to cook uncovered for about 15 minutes, or until the fruit begins to brown.

3. Pour the mixture into the bowl of a food processor and pulse several times, until the sauce is smooth.

4. Allow the sauce to cool to 115°F before adding the honey.

5. Serve warm or cold. Refrigerate any remaining sauce for future use.

Cook's Note: When peaches are not in season, use sliced frozen peaches with no added sugar. Peaches frozen at the height of the season are flavorful, and make a very good substitute for fresh peaches. Fresh pineapples are generally available year-round, but if they are too pricey in the colder months, substitute canned, crushed pineapple with no added sugar.

Fruity Glaze

This sweet, tart glaze livens up any chicken dish. Try painting some on broiled or baked chicken about 10 minutes before the chicken is done cooking.

Prep time: 10 minutes

Makes: about ½ cup

½ cup Raspberry Syrup (page 255) or Cran-Raspberry Sauce (page 256)

2 teaspoons mustard

1½ tablespoons tamari

2 tablespoons orange juice or pineapple juice

1 small clove garlic, crushed

1 teaspoon onion powder

¼ teaspoon sea salt

¼ teaspoon freshly ground black pepper

1. Combine all the ingredients in a small saucepan. Cook over high heat for about 2 minutes, or until the sauce comes to a boil. Lower the heat to medium and simmer for 5 minutes, or until the sauce thickens.

2. Paint the glaze on broiled, baked or grilled chicken during the last 5 minutes of cooking.

Cook's Note: Cooking with fruit adds nutrition, flavor and variety to your dishes. Use this basic glaze as is, or replace the raspberry syrup with pureed peaches or cooked, pureed cherries.

Guacamole

Guacamole is usually served as a dip, but here are a few off-beat serving ideas: put some guacamole on your eggs in the morning, over fresh garden tomatoes for lunch, or on the side of your Sloppy Joes (page 182) for dinner.

Prep time: 15 minutes

Makes: about 1½ cups

2 small, ripe avocados

½ lime, juiced

1½ teaspoons sea salt

¼ teaspoon cumin

1 small clove garlic, minced

1 tablespoon chopped jalapeño pepper

2 tablespoons chopped red onion

2 ripe Roma or cherry tomatoes, seeded and chopped

2 teaspoons chopped cilantro or parsley

1. Cut the avocados in half and scoop out the pulp. Add some of the lime juice and toss until the pulp is coated, so the avocado won't darken in color.

2. Add the salt and cumin, and mash the avocado with a fork.

3. Combine the rest of the lime juice and the remaining ingredients, and stir them into the avocado.

4. Allow the guacamole to sit at room temperature for about an hour before serving, to allow the flavors to blend.

Nutrition Note: Avocado is a rich source of vitamins B6 and E, potassium and healthy essential fatty acids and glutathione. It also contains both monounsaturated and polyunsaturated fats, and it acts as a "nutrient booster" by enabling the body to absorb more fat-soluble nutrients, such as alpha- and beta-carotene and lutein, in other foods that are ingested along with the avocado.

Peach and Blackberry Chutney

Dress up broiled meats and poultry with this chutney made from summer fruits. It tastes sweet, tart and spicy – three flavors all rolled into one.

Prep time: 15 minutes
Cook time: 28 minutes

....

Makes: about 1½ cups

....

1 tablespoon extra virgin olive oil

3 scallions, white part only, chopped

1 clove garlic, crushed

1 teaspoon freshly chopped ginger

3 ripe peaches, peeled and chopped

1 cup blackberries

⅓ cup raisins

¼ cup orange juice

½ teaspoon sea salt

¼ teaspoon freshly ground black pepper

1 tablespoon raw honey

1. Heat the oil in a small saucepan over medium-high heat for 1 minute, or until hot.

2. Sauté the scallions for about 2 minutes, or until they are limp.

3. Add the garlic and ginger, and sauté for 1 minute.

4. Add all the remaining ingredients, except for the honey, and bring the mixture to a boil. Cover the pan, lower the heat, and simmer for 20 minutes.

5. Allow the chutney to cool to 115ºF before adding the honey.

6. Refrigerate and serve cold.

Cook's Note: Chutney can be made with dried fruits when fresh are not in season. Substitute dried apricots for the peaches and fresh or dried apples for the blackberries.

Spicy Ketchup

Tomatoes are part of the nightshade family of vegetables, so introduce them into your diet slowly, because they can cause inflammation (see page 154 for more information). If you have no problem with tomatoes, try this ketchup, which is easy to make and has no preservatives or additives.

Prep time: 5 minutes

Cook time: 2 hours

....

Makes: about 1 quart

....

2 bottles (46 ounces each) tomato juice

¼ cup apple cider vinegar

2 tablespoons tomato paste

1 teaspoon sea salt

2 teaspoons dry mustard

2 teaspoons each onion and garlic powder

1 teaspoon celery salt

1 teaspoon paprika

1 teaspoon ground cumin

½ teaspoon freshly ground black pepper

¼ teaspoon cayenne pepper (optional)

2-4 tablespoons raw honey

1. Place all the ingredients, except for the honey, in a 4-quart saucepot and stir well. Bring the mixture to a boil over medium-high heat. Lower the heat to medium and simmer for 2 hours, or until the mixture is thick.

2. Allow the ketchup to cool for about 30 minutes before stirring in the honey.

3. Refrigerate.

Cook's Note: Prepare this recipe at the beginning of Phase 3, as there are several recipes that call for it, and if you have some already made, it will save you time. If you prefer milder ketchup, eliminate the cayenne pepper and use half the amount of black pepper specified.

Horseradish Mustard Sauce

Use this sauce on sandwiches, or with broiled beef. Be aware that it has a bit of a kick to it.

Prep time: 15 minutes

Makes: 1 cup

½ cup freshly grated horseradish root

2 tablespoons stone ground mustard

1 teaspoon onion powder

1 teaspoon garlic powder

½ teaspoon sea salt

½ cup Homemade Mayonnaise (page 248)

¼ teaspoon freshly ground black pepper

1½ teaspoons raw apple cider vinegar

1 teaspoon raw honey

1. Combine all the ingredients in a bowl.
2. Refrigerate for several hours before using.
3. Refrigerate any leftover sauce.

Cook's Note: Either buy pre-ground horseradish in a jar, or grind it yourself. To grind it in a food processor, cut the root into small pieces to make the processing easier. The fumes are very strong, so be careful not to inhale as you remove the cover from the processor. Leftover ground horseradish freezes very well.

Tartar Sauce

If you have left-over fish, why not make a sandwich topped with lettuce, a slice of tomato and a dollop of tartar sauce?

Prep time: 5 minutes

Makes: about 1 cup

1 recipe's worth
  Homemade Mayonnaise
  (page 248)

3 tablespoons chopped
  pickles

½ teaspoon mustard

1. Combine all the ingredients and stir well.

2. Refrigerate.

Cook's Note: Once you reach Phase 3, you can add a tablespoon or two of Spicy Ketchup (page 271) to make Thousand Island dressing.

Resources

Healthy Eating

Retailers
These retailers carry mostly natural and organic foods.
Whole Foods – www.wholefoodsmarket.com
Trade Joes – www.traderjoes.com

Closeout Stores
Closeout stores can be a great place to find organic foods at a highly discounted price.
Ocean State Job Lot – www.oceanstatejoblot.com
Big Lots – www.biglots.com
TJ Maxx – www.tjmaxx.com
Home Goods – www.homegoods.com

Online Vendors
Bob's Red Mill Natural Foods produces more than 400 products, including a full line of certified gluten-free products and an extensive line of certified organic products. Products can be found in grocery and natural foods stores, or online.
www.bobsredmill.com

Apitherapy raw honey is unheated and unfiltered and can be bought in bulk.
www.honeygardens.com

Eden Foods makes a variety of mustards using raw apple cider vinegar. They also have a large line of wonderful organic foods that can be found in many natural food stores.
www.edenfoods.com

Vital Choice is a good resource for wild Alaskan seafood and organic fare. Food is packed in dry ice before shipping, to keep it frozen and fresh during delivery.
www.vitalchoice.com

Vitacost.com offers wholesale prices on vitamins and supplements, and also on a large selection of organic food and grocery items, such as herbs, honey, xylitol and much more. Some of the best prices can be found on this site.
www.vitacost.com

Vitamin Shoppe is a storefront, but can also be shopped online. They run a lot of great promotions on organic foods and have very good prices all around.
vitaminshoppe.com

Amazon sells a lot more than just books. Many organic food and grocery products can be found here. Just do a search and see if one of their independent sellers has what you are looking for.
www.amazon.com

Mountain Rose Herbs has a wide variety of bulk organic foods, including herbs, spices, extracts, teas and more. Check out the monthly specials tab for extra savings.
www.mountainroseherbs.com

Donna Gate's, proprietor of Body Ecology, sells cow and goat milk, coconut water culture starter kits and many other wonderful products. Already fermented coconut water (coconut kefir) can be bought on this site, as well the sweeteners Lakanto and stevia.
www.bodyecology.com

Online Resources
Local Harvest and Food Routes are two nation-wide organizations that provide directories to assist in finding local community supported agricultures (CSAs), sources for organic foods, food co-ops, natural food stores, sources of raw honey and dairy, grass-fed meats and much more.
www.localharvest.org
www.foodroutes.org

Northeast Organic Farming Association, New Hampshire Chapter (NOFA-NH): This organization provides support for and education in all aspects of organic agriculture.
www.nofanh.org; www.nofanh.org/whybuyorganic

Organic Trade Association (OTA) works to protect organic trade, and envisions organic products becoming a significant part of everyday life, to the benefit of people's lives and the environment.
http://ota.com/

The **USDA** has a comprehensive directory of farmers' markets nationwide. To find one near you, visit the following site.
www.ams.usda.gov/farmersmarkets

Weston A. Price Foundation is dedicated to "restoring nutrient-dense foods to the American diet through education, research and activism." It's a resource for whole and traditional foods and has many articles on a variety of health- and nutrition-related topics.
www.westonaprice.org

Nutrition-Related Reading
Nourishing Traditions: The Cookbook that Challenges Politically Correct Nutrition and the Diet Dictocrats, by Sally Fallon, with Mary G. Enig, Ph.D.
Real Food: What We Eat and Why, by Nina Plank
In Defense of Food: An Eater's Manifesto, by Michael Pollan

Lyme Disease

Organizations
International Lyme and Associated Diseases Society (ILADS) is a nonprofit, international, multi-disciplinary medical society, dedicated to the diagnosis and appropriate treatment of Lyme disease and other tick-borne diseases.
www.ilads.org

Lyme Disease Foundation, Inc. (LDF) is a nonprofit dedicated to finding solutions for tick-borne disorders.
www.lyme.org

Lyme Disease Association (LDA) is an organization dedicated to Lyme disease education, prevention, research funding, and patient support.
www.lymediseaseassociation.org

Lyme Disease Association of Southeastern Pennsylvania has some very valuable information on their website; most notably, the downloadable, free publication *Lyme Disease and associated tick-borne diseases: The Basics*, which is in its fifth edition.
www.lymepa.org

Movies and Books
Under Our Skin, produced by Open Eye Pictures, is the highly-acclaimed documentary that exposes the hidden story of Lyme disease – one of the most controversial and fastest growing epidemics of our time.
www.openeyepictures.com

Healing Lyme, by Stephen Harrod Buhner
Coping with Lyme Disease, by Denise Lang, with Kenneth Liegner, MD
The Lyme Disease Solution, by Kenneth B. Singleton, MD
Insights into Lyme Disease Treatment, by Connie Strasheim
The Lyme Survival Guide, by Connie Strasheim
Everything You Need to Know About Lyme Disease and Other Tick-Borne Disorders, by Karen Vanderhoof-Forschner
Cure Unknown, by Pamela Weintraub

Index

About the Authors

Gail Piazza has been a successful home economics consultant for over thirty years. In addition to authoring a cookbook herself (*The World of Wok Cookery*), she has also collaborated on a half-dozen other cookbooks; developed, adapted or tested recipes for numerous projects and clients; worked with small appliance designers to refine and test their products; and provided props and styled food for movies and television commercials. Her extensive list of clients includes All-Clad, Emerilware, Krups, Farberware and Hamilton Beach/Proctor-Silex Inc.

Laura Piazza is an award-winning Certified Professional Photographer and graphic designer. She is the the co-owner of the high-end wedding photography business, Natural Expressions Wedding Photography, LLC (www.naturalexpressions-photo.com), and primarily works as a wedding and commercial photographer. Additionally, she has created thousands of design projects for a variety of employers and clients. In her free time, she does landscape, abstract and portrait photography. More of her work can be viewed at www.piazzacreative.com.